The Stoic Man's Guide

Daily Strategies for Modern Men: How to
Embrace Timeless Stoicism for
Happiness, Resilience, and Well-Being

William T. Harrison

A Personal Note from the Author

Dear Cherished Reader,

From the bottom of my heart, I want to express my sincerest gratitude for bringing this book into your life. I hope that the stories, insights, and emotions within these pages resonate with you and add something meaningful to your day.

Writing this book has been a journey filled with passion, reflection, and discovery, and I am thrilled to share it with you. Your support means everything to me, and I am profoundly grateful for the time you are spending with my words.

I believe in the power of shared stories and experiences, and I am eager to hear your thoughts on this book. If you could take a moment to leave an honest review on Amazon, I would immensely appreciate it. Your feedback is invaluable, helping me to grow as a writer and assisting fellow readers in their quest for meaningful reads.

Thank you once again for your support, and for being a vital part of this literary adventure.

With heartfelt thanks and warmest wishes,

William

Table of Contents

Introduction

Think about the problems you are facing in your life. Perhaps you are facing financial difficulties. Perhaps you are having relationship problems, or a family member is unwell. Perhaps it's less serious, and you're having trouble keeping your cool during your daily commute. Write down the first three problems that come to your head, the ones that stop you from living your best life.

Now think about which elements of these problems you can control and which elements you cannot. For example, if a close family member is feeling unwell, this is something that is out of your hands. Unless you are their primary physician, or otherwise directly involved in their state of health, it falls beyond your power to make them well.

However, there are elements of the situation that you can control. You have influence over how you react to them being unwell. You can control whether you offer them help or whether you are an additional burden upon them. You can also control, to some extent, whether the news of their sickness is debilitating to your own life or whether it inspires you to take proactive steps to improve the situation.

Recognizing the difference between those elements you can control and those you can't is a practice that lies at the heart of the philosophy of Stoicism. Though the philosophy is truly ancient—going back to around 300 B.C.E. and the Ancient Greeks—its lessons are wildly applicable to modern life. In fact, there is an argument to be made that Stoicism is more relevant today than ever.

The ancient Stoics lived lives that were more under their control. They did not face the pressures and influences of global capitalism, market forces, or a worldwide Internet: Forces that constantly affect our lives in a manner we have no hope of controlling. Whether or not we can afford our mortgages depends not only on our personal financial conduct but also on the state of the stock market, oil prices, and global economies.

An interconnected, truly global world brings many benefits, but it also brings home that there are important facets of our lives that fall beyond our control. By applying the tenets of Stoicism to these modern challenges, you can meet these obstacles head-on. You can maintain a sense of inner contentment and satisfaction, or what the ancient Stoics called *eudaemonia*.

The philosophy of Stoicism began with Zeno of Citium. Like many of the ancient Stoics, Zeno faced disaster in his life and turned to philosophy as a way to rise above those challenges and persevere. Before he founded the school of Stoicism—named for the porch, or *Stoa Poikilê*, at which the first Stoics met—Zeno was a merchant. Yet on the voyage from Phoenicia to Peiraeus, he suffered a shipwreck and lost almost everything. Instead of succumbing to despair, Zeno founded a new philosophy: Stoicism. This philosophy would be incredibly influential, finding proponents in former slaves such as Epictetus, Roman senators such as Seneca, as well as emperors such as Marcus Aurelius.

Stoicism is often equated with the attitude of having a stiff upper lip: never admitting weakness or hardship and rising above any trial. Though there are some comparisons to be made, the truth is that Stoicism is not about denying your basic humanity but embracing it.

Stoicism does not ask you to pretend that you don't have emotions but instead asks you to recognize the value of living in harmony with nature and living your life in a virtuous manner to achieve inner flourishing. It is a philosophy of how to live life well, and, though it will empower you to meet challenges with courage and wisdom, it is more about understanding your nature than denying it.

I am more than just the author of this book. I am someone who practices the philosophy of Stoicism in daily life. My journey into Stoicism began in my 30s, after the unexpected passing of my close friend and business partner. I don't mind admitting that I needed the help that Stoicism could offer. I was personally devastated by the death of my friend, which, combined with the subsequent collapse of our joint business venture, left me feeling directionless. I searched for answers and a way to rebuild, and I found the timeless wisdom of Stoicism. I found solace and guidance in its principles of living virtuously, building inner resilience, and practicing mindfulness.

What began as a personal quest for understanding soon blossomed into a lifelong passion for sharing the transformative power of Stoic philosophy. I believe in the wisdom of Stoicism because I have lived it. Though it is not easy—it may be impossible—to be the *perfect* Stoic, I strive every day to live according to those ideals.

It has helped me stay strong through moments of immense challenge, empowering me not to bottle or repress how I feel but to face those emotions directly and react in a manner that shows courage and temperance. It has helped me to be the best father and committed family man I can be. It has helped me act virtuously in a world that often tempts us to do the wrong thing, and it has led me to an inner peace and sense of self-respect that is hard-won but entirely worth the effort.

If you are struggling or looking for answers, then this is the book for you. By picking up this book and thinking about how to live a better life, you have already shown courage: You have recognized dissatisfaction with your life and sought out a way to fix that problem directly. You have shown humility, wisdom, and profound self-honesty, all of which are hallmarks of a Stoic life. Even if things are tough right now, you have demonstrated that you have the strength and internal sense of justice to make things better. That's not nothing. In fact, that's something to be proud of.

There is one thing I want to make clear at the outset: The life of a Stoic is not always easy, and it is not binary. You can't just flip a switch and become the perfect Stoic. Stoicism is a way of living, and like all things worth doing, it takes practice, hard work, and determination. Don't allow yourself to be demotivated by small setbacks or bumps in the road. Grit your teeth, think about how those challenges can be overcome, and keep going. One day soon, you'll look at your life and realize that you are happier and more resilient, even if you can't identify when precisely that came to be.

This book is split into four parts. The first part introduces you to the philosophy of Stoicism in a bit more detail and builds the principle of the new Stoic man. In the second part, we talk about how Stoicism can be applied to your daily life, looking at techniques for practicing Stoicism as well as thinking about everyday issues and your personal relationships. From there, in the third part, we think about how Stoicism connects to your personal growth, considering different aspects of your health, from the physical to the spiritual. The fourth and final part considers contemporary issues of the modern world and discusses how the philosophy of Stoicism can be applied to these new challenges.

Part 1:

Stoicism and the Modern Man

Keep this thought handy when you feel a fit of rage coming on—it isn't manly to be enraged. Rather, gentleness and humility are more human, and therefore manlier. A real man doesn't give way to anger and discontent and such a person has strength, courage, and endurance—unlike the angry and complaining. The nearer a man comes to a calm mind, the closer he is to strength. –Marcus Aurelius

You are in traffic on your daily commute to work. The traffic is slow moving. Someone cuts in front of you. What should a man do?

As a society, we tend to have a stereotypical notion of a man being aggressive, assertive, and confrontational. According to this depiction of masculinity, a man might hit his horn, shake his fist, or even get out of his car and start a physical altercation. But this is not the ideal of masculinity that Stoicism advocates.

First and foremost, Stoicism teaches that a man is rational and temperate. A man does not let animal impulses get the better of him and immediately act out like a snarling dog when he is wronged. A true man is better than that. *We* are better than that.

So, let's suppose that you are on the way to work, facing heavy traffic. Someone cuts in front of you. By the Stoic ideal of masculinity, you don't shout, wave your fist, or hit the horn. You recognize that displays of aggression will not make the world better and that there is no wisdom in aggression that achieves nothing but aggression in itself.

You remain temperate and in control of your emotions. You apply the tenets of justice and recognize that getting upset is not just: It simply punishes you more by upsetting you. Instead, you face your emotions head-on, recognize your frustration and distress, and demonstrate courage by confronting those feelings honestly and directly. And, in keeping cool and rising above, you show yourself and the world that you are a good man.

In Part 1, we will examine what it is to be a modern man living to the ideals of Stoicism. In Chapter 1, we will consider the nine tenets of Stoicism, supplementing these tenets with a discussion of the four cardinal virtues (wisdom, courage, justice, and temperance) in Chapter 2. From there, in Chapter 3, we will apply these tenets and virtues to consider how a modern man should behave when living a Stoic life.

Chapter 1:

The Nine Tenets of Stoicism

This chapter describes the nine tenets of Stoicism by which you can start to live a better, more fulfilling life.

In truth, there is no set of commandments or list of rules that exhaust the principles of Stoicism. Different authorities may cite only eight or as many as twelve basic tenets. However, all summaries of Stoicism tend to include the nine outlined in this chapter. As such, learning and internalizing these tenets is an excellent start to understanding what it is to live a Stoic life.

When reading these tenets, it is worth remembering from the outset what philosophy was to the Ancient Greeks. Modern philosophy tends to be very focused on specific problems, such as whether we have free will or what it is for one event to cause another. For the Ancient Greeks, however, philosophy was the study of how to live well. Stoicism is not about providing technical answers to metaphysical questions but about living according to best principles and flourishing in our inner lives.

Tenet 1: Live According to Nature

A fundamental principle of Stoicism is that, as humans, we are rational animals. To live according to our nature, then, we must embrace our inner rationality and apply it to the way we live.

This idea has many implications. First, it means that we should not act impulsively on animal passions. An animal may eat when it is hungry, drink when it is thirsty, or bolt when it is frightened. However, for us as rational beings, there should be a step between those emotions and our actions: a step of deliberate selection.

There is nothing innately wrong with eating when you are hungry, in the absence of other considerations. But the world is a complex place. You may be hungry, but there might not be enough food to go around. Instead of eating immediately—in the manner of a greedy dog, for example—we should instead live according to our nature and apply our reason. If there is not enough food to go around, we should determine what action would be virtuous, whether it would be just for us to eat or whether we should let the food go to someone else.

When understanding Stoicism, it's important to remember that the ancient Stoics thought that virtue was the epitome of reason. The Stoics were concerned with the knowledge of how to live well and considered virtuous living to be the answer. As such, to live according to our nature—to live according to our innate reason—we must consider how to act virtuously when confronted with our appetites and fears. We will discuss the four virtues in more detail in Chapter 2.

Secondly, for us to live according to nature is to recognize what is appropriate for ourselves. The ancient Stoics had a word for actions that both accorded with one's nature and were justified by reason: *kathékon,* or "a proper function." This requires both understanding ourselves on a biological level, as well as on a moral level. For example, eating too much and becoming unhealthy is not living according to our proper nature on a biological level.

On the other hand, we must also consider the moral component and recognize that our personal health is not to be pursued to the exclusion of all else. Sometimes, virtue asks us to risk our health. For example, when we must put ourselves in harm's way to help another human being, or (returning to the previous example) when we must go hungry so others can eat.

The first tenet of Stoicism, then, asks us to recognize that we are both animals and rational. We must understand what is appropriate for the animal being, but we must also understand what is virtuous so that we can live according to our proper nature.

Tenet 2: Fulfillment Is Not Found in Things but in Actions and Virtuous Living

The ancient Stoics, in their pursuit of the knowledge of how to live well, were concerned with finding the truly good. They believed that true good would bring fulfillment, or eudaemonia. Moreover, they believed that true good could not be conditional: It had to be something that was good regardless of the circumstances.

This led the Stoics to think about virtues because other things that are good can become bad in excess or in certain circumstances. Consider, for example, wealth. Wealth is good because it brings comfort and the opportunity to partake in enjoyable experiences. However, wealth cannot be considered a true good because there are circumstances in which it might lead you to ruin. Take, for example, a heroin addict. If a heroin addict suddenly came into great wealth, they would use that money to buy heroin and destroy their bodies. Consequently, wealth cannot be truly good because the true good is never bad.

By contrast, there is no circumstance in which it is bad to act virtuously. In Chapter 2, we will discuss the four cardinal virtues of Stoicism: courage, justice, temperance, and wisdom. By their very nature, there is no circumstance in which it is bad to act courageously, or with wisdom, and so on. As such, the true good is virtuous living and all else follows from that.

Meanwhile, virtue is not a passive thing. As we have already discussed, Stoicism holds that human beings have reason. This means that we are not simply input and output. Our actions are not the result of automatic processes following some external stimuli. If we live according to our nature, we apply reason to decide how to act. And, because we are concerned with living a good life and finding fulfillment, reason is all about selecting the true good.

Putting this all together: Reason is about selecting which action is most virtuous. This means that fulfillment lies not in things but in our actions. By choosing the action that is most virtuous, we live our best lives. Living our best lives leads to contentment and fulfillment: It leads to eudaemonia.

Tenet 3: We Cannot Control External Events, Only Our Opinions, Choices, Thoughts, and Actions

More than ever, we are affected by external events that we cannot control. Global market forces determine our cost of living and whether we struggle financially. Pandemics that begin on one continent can reach our country through the miracles of international travel. We live in an interconnected world, which means that we are acted on by external events every second of every day.

If we are struggling or facing hardships, it can be easy to want to tackle the problem at its source. However, Stoicism holds that you should resist this impulse. Unless you have reached a position of extraordinary influence, there is little wisdom in attempting to undo global capitalism. You simply will not succeed, and you will expend a lot of energy in the meantime. Furthermore, even if you did succeed, would your hardship go away? Often, the external events that cause us hardship or difficulty have already happened. We cannot change the past.

Instead, Stoicism asks us to consider what we *can* control. As Marcus Aurelius famously wrote, "If you are pained by any external thing, it is not this thing that disturbs you, but your own judgment about it. And it is in your power to wipe out this judgment now" (Aurelius, 2006/161–180 A.D.).

We cannot control external events, but we can control how we react. Of course, this may have some limits. For example, pain feels unpleasant, and there's not much we can do about that. We can, however, choose how we act in response to that pain. We can decide to respond with courage and fortitude and to act in a virtuous manner. As it happens, choosing to react virtuously goes a long way in making our struggles more bearable.

Tenet 4: We Have the Tools to Thrive

Because fulfillment is found in virtuous action, it follows that everyone, regardless of the circumstances of their birth, can find happiness and thrive.

Epictetus, one of the most famous ancient Stoics, was a slave. He later became a free man, but he did not forget the lessons he had learned in slavery. He continued to live humbly, focusing on principled living rather than the acquisition of more and more possessions. He thrived despite his hardships.

Stoicism, at its heart, has an "optimistic view of the human personality" (Hanselman, n.d.). It holds that all human beings are connected by their reason and capacity for virtue. Regardless of their circumstances or hardships, all human beings can choose to react in a way that is honorable. Regardless of whether you are poor, unwell, or otherwise disadvantaged, you can choose to act with courage, justice, temperance, and wisdom. And, because fulfillment and thriving come from virtuous action, not from things, it follows that all human beings can thrive—from slave, in the case of Epictetus, to Roman Emperor, in the case of Marcus Aurelius.

Tenet 5: *Apatheia*: Eliminate Negative Emotions and Overreactions

Stoicism is often mistaken as a philosophy for robots. Sometimes, people think that Stoicism asks us to suppress or deny our basic emotions. However, this is not the case. Stoicism holds that we should be constantly reflecting on our emotions and feelings and working with them rather than against them.

However, Stoicism does teach that we should be careful about overindulging in toxic sentiments. Our first emotional responses are often untouched by reason and are animalistic. If we overindulge in these reactions and allow them to guide how we act, this can lead to negative outcomes.

The Stoics held that we should seek to control or curb those impulses that work in opposition to reason. For example, uncontrolled desire or fear can make it difficult for us to be rational, driving us toward or away from what we desire or fear without much thought of virtue. Yet the solution is not just to repress that desire or fear, but to channel it into more temperate emotions. We might seek to channel desire into wishing and fear into caution, for instance. This allows us to acknowledge our emotions and feelings without letting them dominate how we react and behave.

There is nothing wrong with being cautious about wasting money. This caution works with our innate reason, helping us to make prudent financial decisions and to avoid intemperate waste. However, if we are too fearful, this leads to miserly and uncharitable actions and prevents us from flourishing. Emotions are fine, but they should work in tandem with virtue and reason rather than drowning them.

Tenet 6: Rationality in the World and in Ourselves: Accept Responsibility

A corollary of accepting that we cannot control external events is recognizing that we do control how we react to them. This means that we should demonstrate moral courage in accepting responsibility for how we choose to act and learning from our errors when we fall short.

This does not mean that you have to castigate yourself whenever you make a mistake. As a human being, you will sometimes fall short of the Stoic ideals. You will be tempted away from virtuous action by intemperate desires or shy away from the right thing due to fear.

Sometimes, you will lose your temper or act rashly. Stoicism does not ask you to fall on your sword, but it does ask you to accept responsibility and examine what went wrong.

A huge part of the tradition of Stoicism is the idea of self-reflection. The Roman senator and Stoic, Lucius Seneca, wrote, "This is what makes us evil—that none of us looks back upon our own lives" (2017/c.65 A.D.). However, to learn from our mistakes and apply the benefits of self-reflection, we must first accept that we made mistakes and show a radical honesty that allows for awareness of our errors. In short, we must accept responsibility for our misdeeds.

Tenet 7: No Man Is an Island: We Are Part of the World

The noun *cosmopolitan* has its origins in Epictetus and means "a person of the world." This idea—that we should be people of the world rather than isolated islands—is a fundamentally Stoic principle.

Part of this comes from Stoicism's profound optimism about human nature. We are all connected by our innate capacity for virtue and rationality, and it is therefore in accordance with our proper nature that we should have fellowship with other human beings. It is a fact of human nature that we benefit from a sense of community, and thus, it is an act of wisdom to accept our role in the world.

The idea of becoming a cosmopolitan also follows from living virtuously. For example, the virtue of justice does not make much sense if you are an island. Living justly involves recognizing your place in society and doing your bit to improve the fairness of that society through your actions.

What was true in the time of the ancient Stoics is only truer today: We live in an inextricably interconnected world. When we post something on the Internet, it can be read by people in different countries or even on different continents. When we purchase a cup of coffee, we might be contributing to unfair working practices hundreds of miles away or otherwise helping to support fair trade practices across the world. Whether you like it or not, no man is an island. Consequently, to live virtuously is to accept your part in the world and to act accordingly.

Tenet 8: We Can Only Grow When We Are Part of Something Greater

As noted, Stoicism holds that we live as part of the world. The human species has achieved great things through co-operation, and it is to live according to our rational nature that we should embrace our part in something greater than ourselves.

Fundamentally, it is important to show humility when seeking wisdom. As Epictetus wrote, "It is impossible for a man to learn what he thinks he already knows" (2008/c.108 A.D.). If we do not accept that we are part of something greater, we will remain ignorant of how we might live better and more honorably.

Humility can be difficult. Ultimately, it requires moral courage and wisdom to recognize our limits and to understand that we are but a small part of the cosmos. However, humility is a prerequisite to a reasoned, virtuous life, and thus necessary for you to achieve the fulfillment of eudaemonia.

Tenet 9: Progress, Not Perfection

Finally, it is important to remember that the ideal Stoic life is just that: an ideal.

For the ancient Stoics, philosophy was not a mere academic discipline. It was not something that could be studied simply in books but something that had to be practiced in daily life. Living according to the virtues of Stoicism is not always easy, and sometimes you are going to fall short. You are going to be intemperate on occasion. You are going to act foolishly, or unjustly, or avoid something that you should have tackled head-on. That is okay.

Stoicism is not a stick to beat yourself with. It is a route to better living, and you do not complete a journey in a single step. The important thing is recognizing where you fall short, thinking about what steps you can make to avoid similar errors in the future, and persevering. It is enough to simply progress. Don't let perfection be the enemy of good.

It is, fundamentally, about self-respect. Accept that you make mistakes but that you are trying. Struggle manfully and try to be a better person. Treat yourself with honesty and courage, accept responsibility for your actions, and you will be on the path to a better, more virtuous life.

Chapter 2:

The Four Virtues

WISDOM | COURAGE | JUSTICE | TEMPERANCE

The Stoics believed that the true good should be good in all instances. As we discussed in the previous chapter, the ancient Stoics believed that the only true good was the virtues. This is because there is no circumstance in which it is bad to be virtuous.

This chapter will outline the four cardinal virtues proposed by the philosophy of Stoicism: wisdom, courage, justice, and temperance. By trying to act in accordance with these virtues, you can start becoming a better man and flourish as a result. As Marcus Aurelius wrote: "If at some point in your life, you should come across anything better than justice, wisdom, discipline, courage—it must be an extraordinary thing indeed" (2006/161-180 A.D.).

Wisdom

Some writers claim that wisdom is the overarching virtue from which all others derive. After all, it is wise to show courage, temperance, and justice.

Wisdom is tricky to define but can be recognized by its aspects. These include thinking logically, being emotionally intelligent, understanding yourself and others, and achieving a balanced view of any situation. It is the willingness to apply reason to a situation rather than rushing in with an emotional response. It also involves humility and accepting that, sometimes, it may be better to listen than to speak. One of the more important facets of wisdom is the third tenet of Stoicism: recognizing the limits of what you can control. Let's consider an example. A close relative is very unwell. They are receiving medical care but their prognosis is not positive. You must decide how to react and what to do in this instance.

A very common response to this kind of situation is to desperately seek miracle cures on the Internet. The reason that this course of action is unwise is because it fails to recognize the limits of your control. Unless you are a doctor, you will not know better than the professionals already caring for your relative. By seeking miracle cures from random websites, you are grasping for control over a situation that lies beyond your power.

Let's consider how you might react to this situation with the benefit of wisdom. You recognize that you are not in a position to heal your relative. You identify what lies within your control and what does not.

This does not mean that you are entirely powerless to improve the situation. You might not have power over your relative's health, but you can offer comfort and support. You can improve the situation by being there for them. By applying wisdom, you can identify where best to apply your energies and do your bit to make a bad situation more bearable.

As noted, wisdom is also connected to humility: the idea that sometimes you might not be in possession of all the facts. Let's consider another example. You are at work and a colleague—who is normally entirely pleasant—snaps at you over a minor error. How do you react?

It might be natural to react with hurt or else defend yourself with a harsh comment in return. After all, your colleague has acted in a way that is unreasonable, and it is natural to want to defend yourself. However, by practicing wisdom, you might get a more rounded view of the matter. First of all, you may recognize that there is nothing to be gained in making a bad situation worse. Your colleague's rudeness does not represent a pattern of behavior that needs addressing, so escalating an unpleasant moment into a full argument is unwise and thus unmanly.

Second of all, you might apply wisdom to consider that your colleague's rudeness may not be about you at all. People are often abrasive because they are having a bad day. It is not a positive trait (and something worth working on if you tend to act this way), but it is a common pattern of human behavior.

By taking a moment to think about the issue, you will find the insight to recognize that something must be going on in your colleague's day that has put them in a bad mood. This will help you not to take the slight personally and to respond in a way that is positive and productive. Maybe you will respond to their rudeness with kindness and try to make their day a little better. Through wisdom, you will be a force for good rather than further negativity.

Courage

Courage is the virtue of standing up for what is right, even if it might materially disadvantage or inconvenience you to do so. It is standing by your principles rather than compromising for a short-term advantage. It is integrity.

Modifying the example from the previous section, let us suppose that your colleague is constantly rude toward you and others. They belittle your work, act superior to their peers, and sneer at any idea that is not theirs.

Many people would choose to ignore their behavior on the basis of avoiding confrontation and its unpleasantness. However, courage asks you to stand up for yourself and address the situation calmly but firmly. You should address your colleague's behavior as a fellow rational human being and establish your boundaries without escalating the issue into a shouting match.

This example does not mean that courage is about seeking confrontation—far from it, in fact. It just means that you should not shy away from confrontation when it is necessary. To demonstrate this point, let's think about a situation where courage would lead you to avoid confrontation. For instance, it can take courage to confront your own limitations head-on. If you have a temper, admitting that to yourself can be difficult and scary. By having courage and taking steps to honestly identify and address your shortcomings, you may put into place measures that prevent the need for confrontations in the future.

Courage, then, is not the same as aggression. It is radical self-honesty—even when that honesty may not feel flattering—and self-respect. This means holding fast to your principles and addressing your shortcomings. Sticking by your principles may feel isolating in some moments, but this is when it is most important to find your courage.

Suppose that you are at a hangout with your friends, and everyone is picking on a mutual acquaintance. They are making snide comments and insults. In short, their behavior is approaching bullying. We all know that this behavior is wrong, but very few people have the courage to stick their neck out for a relative stranger and make things awkward with their friends.

That does not mean that it isn't virtuous to stand up for the person and take a stand against bullying where you see it. It may feel unpleasant in the moment, but this pales against the sense of self-respect you will feel in the long run, knowing that you are a man of principle. You will know that you are the kind of person who does the right thing, even when it is not easy.

Justice

The third cardinal virtue of Stoicism is justice—that is, fairness and equity. Living according to justice means not taking more than your fair share and also contributing to your society in a way that does not unfairly disadvantage others while advantaging yourself.

When most people think of justice, they often think about politics and the justice of tax systems, penal codes, or social securities. This is an important part of justice, but this virtue is not exhausted by lofty principles of governance and ethics. Everyday life provides many opportunities to demonstrate integrity: from making sure that your quieter colleague gets full credit for their great idea to simply not eating all the snacks that are meant to be shared around the whole office. At home, it means contributing to household chores in an equitable manner and making sure that your partner's needs are met as well as your own.

Like with all the virtues, justice can be inconvenient to your short-term interests. After all, there are advantages to taking all the credit for a group project. There are benefits to always getting your own way and always getting to do what you want to do. However, these joys are short-lived, short term, and diminish your sense of self.

You might get the credit from your boss or teacher, but you will have missed out on fellowship with your peers. You will also know deep down that your success is built on dishonesty and moral weakness. You might trick your partner or housemates into doing all the chores, but your relationships will not be built on trust and mutual co-operation, and they will suffer as a result. Ultimately, living virtuously may not provide an immediate benefit, but it is a better way to live in the long run, helping you build lasting relationships and a lasting sense of self-respect.

Justice also means taking responsibility for your actions and taking steps to make amends for any wrongdoing. This can range from a simple apology to a more serious confession. For example, if you weren't paying attention and you cut someone off in traffic, this virtue demands that you offer a wave of apology. Meanwhile, if in a moment of weakness, you "borrowed" your housemate's car and scratched the bumper, living justly means that you come clean and pay for the repairs.

Similarly, justice might involve you swallowing your pride and accepting your share of responsibility in an argument. If you catch yourself acting unreasonably, do not stick to your position for the sake of your ego. Instead, back down and do what is right. It is more manly to recognize your errors than to stick by them in defense of a fragile ego.

Temperance

You have probably heard the phrase "all things in moderation." This idea is at the heart of the virtue of temperance: to avoid excesses and to be measured in all things.

Temperance applies to many different matters. On one hand, temperance calls for not overindulging at the buffet table or recognizing your limit before you go to get another drink. On the other hand, it means not overindulging in toxic emotions that can lead you astray. In Chapter 1, we talked about how Stoicism doesn't want you to repress your emotions but instead channel them into more moderate expressions. This is putting temperance into action.

For example, if you are experiencing impulsive feelings of desire for more wealth, temperance involves moderating that into a more measured sense of wishing for wealth. By practicing temperance, you may still strive for better living conditions, but you will not lose all sense of reason in your pursuit of money. In this sense, temperance is about balancing your emotions such that they are still tractable to virtue and reason.

Temperance is therefore about self-control and discipline. Sometimes this will be about curbing your aggression. Remember that, according to Stoicism, it is not manly to fly off the handle and lose your cool. You are a rational being who can exert control over your own behaviors. So, if someone cuts in front of you in line, do not yell at them or shove them. Address the matter politely if you think it is virtuous to do so but remain in control.

Temperance is also very important for maintaining the discipline of habit needed to live a Stoic life. Many aspects of Stoicism require practice, hard work, and dedication. Sometimes it will be tempting to give in and do what feels easier in the moment. Temperance, in the discipline it entails, will be the virtue that gives you strength in these moments of weakness.

Some ancient Stoics saw fit to practice their discipline and resilience through voluntary hardships by purposefully living below their means. They did this to demonstrate to themselves their inner strength. Similarly for the modern Stoic, by practicing temperance in everyday life, you train yourself for more difficult moments and prove to yourself that you have the inner strength to overcome even the greatest hardships.

Chapter 3:

The New Stoic Man

Stoicism is a philosophy with a long tradition. It is over 2,000 years old, and in the span of its existence, there have been modifications and divergences. This is to be expected, and so this chapter lays out a particular concept of the new Stoic man that differs from some modern interpretations of Stoicism. In particular, the Stoicism outlined in this chapter does not ask for emotionless self-control, simply for mental resilience to endure tough times. According to this conception of Stoicism, a man may do the right thing without sacrificing his emotions as a human being.

Masculinity and Stoicism: A New Vision of Strength

We know that repressing harmful emotions is mentally unhealthy. Repressing emotions tends to empower them and results in men not getting the help they need, whether this be medical care for the treatment of pain or therapy for getting through difficult times. This common-sense observation is also supported by studies: The academic Andrew Moore and his team (2012) found that a stubborn, uncomplaining attitude can result in worse health outcomes for patients.

The truth is, it can take a lot of strength to admit that you need help. It takes courage and wisdom because it involves admitting to yourself that you are struggling and also understanding that you can't fix the problem entirely on your own. There is nothing incompatible between the Stoic mindset and getting therapy. In fact, stubbornly refusing to get help is not Stoic at all: It is unwise and unjust to yourself.

Toxic masculinity has pervaded for long enough and is inconsistent with Stoic principles. A Stoic man has the courage to be his authentic, honest self without worrying about the skewed expectations of others. He holds true to his principles and to who he is, doing what is right regardless of society's pressures. He understands the difference between what he can control and what he cannot, and, crucially, he understands his own nature rather than living in denial for the sake of a stiff upper lip.

As Dr. Myles Spar puts it, "Being a successful and respectable man shouldn't mean hiding emotions and pretending not to need help. It should mean knowing oneself and being authentic, not hiding one's weaknesses" (n.d.).

Challenging Stereotypes

Men are often expected to suffer in silence. We are told to "man up," or "walk it off." However, this is a perversion of manliness. A man handles his problems forthrightly and sensibly. He doesn't bury his head in the sand and pretend that those problems don't exist.

Suppose that you slipped, fell, and broke your leg. There is no virtue in pretending that you have not broken your leg. Standing up without a grimace might involve an extraordinary amount of self-control but pretending that you are not in agony and continuing to walk on the leg is just a good way of ensuring it will not heal properly. There is no wisdom in this course of action. Nor is there temperance. At a certain point, refusing to admit that you need a doctor starts to look a lot like pride. It is not manly to insist on "walking off" a broken leg: It is just dumb.

We accept this in the case of physical injury like broken legs, or physical ailments like cancer, but as men, we tend to have a blind spot when it comes to mental health difficulties. However, the reality is that mental health is part of overall health. Everything I said about walking on broken legs applies equally to ignoring mental health difficulties and refusing to get treatment.

If you are struggling with depression or anxiety, pretending otherwise will only exacerbate those problems and result in you isolating yourself from the world. There is no wisdom in this. Instead, it is worth reaching out to professional therapists that can help you. It will take courage—men have unfortunately been raised to feel uncomfortable about sharing our feelings—but, in seeking help, you prove your manliness and Stoic attitude. There is a problem, and it must be addressed directly with the assistance of experts. When you have identified the problem and tackled it head-on, you will have done so in a way that is sensible and wise.

This is a lesson that can save lives. Benita Chatmon, Assistant Dean for Clinical Nursing Education at the School of Nursing in New Orleans, writes that "depression and suicide are ranked as a leading cause of death among men" (2020). Men die by suicide at a rate four times higher than women, and 62,000 men die per year due to alcohol-related causes compared to 26,000 women. Furthermore, men are between two to three times more likely to misuse drugs than women are. This shows that men are in the habit of trying to self-medicate their problems and go at managing them alone, and it is not working.

The point is so important that it is worth repeating: A man addresses those problems that he has the power to influence. Pretending that you don't have depression, anxiety, or another mental health disorder isn't virtuous. It is ignoring a real issue and avoiding doing something about it. That is not manly, and it is not healthy. Have the courage to address how you are feeling. Have the wisdom to seek expert advice rather than to self-medicate with alcohol or narcotics. Show yourself justice by getting the help you need and deserve as a human being.

Embracing Vulnerability and Emotional Intelligence

Of course, not every problem in life rises to the level of a mental health difficulty. Accepting problems and addressing them directly goes beyond getting a therapist when you are feeling depressed or anxious. Again, the thought is this: A man, as a rational human being, should address issues in his life that he is in a position to control, and he should seek self-understanding and wisdom.

It is a Stoic ideal to have a good understanding of your own nature. This requires developing your emotional intelligence and embracing vulnerability where it exists. Remember that vulnerability—in the sense of expressing our emotions or sentimentalities—is not the same as weakness. It is what it is to be human.

Showing vulnerability to a cat on the street by stopping to pet it is a sign of empathy and kindness. Showing vulnerability to your partner by being radically honest about your feelings is a sign of courage and strength. Showing vulnerability to your friends is an act of true, principled leadership as you are providing an example for others for being in touch with their feelings and avoiding emotional disaster.

Later in this chapter, we will discuss how you might build on your self-awareness and emotional intelligence. First, though, let's think about what emotional intelligence is. Kendra Cherry from VeryWell Mind writes that emotional intelligence "is the ability to perceive, interpret, demonstrate, control, evaluate, and use emotions to communicate with and relate to others effectively and constructively" (2023). In short, it is a form of knowledge and wisdom. It involves recognizing emotions in others and identifying them correctly so that you understand a situation and can take steps to guide that situation to a better outcome.

As men, sometimes we can take a dismissive approach to emotional intelligence. We are told that it is unmanly to be in touch with our emotions, or that men *do* rather than feel. This is cowardly and unwise. It is cowardly because it is just an excuse to bury our heads in the sand rather than face emotional issues directly. It is unwise because we all know that emotions matter. To stubbornly ignore how we feel on the basis of some form of toxic masculinity is just putting us at a disadvantage in a world driven by emotions. There is no virtue in that.

The Stoic Mindset: Building Mental Resilience

It is long known that expressing vulnerability is a path to mental resilience. Being in touch with your feelings and processing them healthily is far better than ignoring them. Otherwise, we become brittle and irritable, unable to process our emotions other than through self-defensive anger.

Mental resilience is best seen as a sponge rather than a wall. It is the ability to absorb emotions and channel them in a productive manner. Despite our best efforts, we men feel. Our inability to process these emotions in a healthy way results in self-soothing behaviors and self-medicating with alcohol and drugs. These "solutions" do not build resilience. Instead, they tend to make the situation worse. Rather, the Stoic man should seek to build his mental resilience using healthy, productive strategies.

The rest of this chapter will consider some mindfulness techniques and other exercises designed to boost your mental resilience. However, it is worth remembering that different forms of resilience are interconnected. In addition to your mental resilience, it is worth thinking about your physical, social, and spiritual resilience.

Physical Resilience

Your physical resilience is, essentially, your health. The writers at Psychology Today note that "healthy habits—getting enough sleep, eating well, and exercising—can reduce stress, which may, in turn, boost resilience" (n.d.). The following tips can be a great start to building your physical resilience, improving your health, and in turn, boosting your mental fortitude:

- **Remove screens from the bedroom:** Resisting the urge to look at your phone in bed can be a big boost for your sleep hygiene. The blue light from phone screens signals to your brain that it's daytime and it should be awake—hardly what you need when you're trying to get to sleep. By avoiding phones in bed, you avoid this issue and also prevent your mind from staying active when it needs to be winding down.

- **Put sleep routines in practice:** You can train your body to fall asleep at certain times through habit and repetition. If you don't already, consider setting yourself a fixed bedtime and morning wake-up point. With repetition, it will help you get to sleep more easily. Don't worry if you sometimes need more flexibility; just stick to the habit whenever it is practical.

- **Look at your diet and cut out snacking:** If you are a little overweight or otherwise have an unhealthy diet, take a look to see if there are some quick fixes for improvement. Cutting out snacking or replacing unhealthy foods with fruit and vegetables can make a big difference to your health and waistline.

- **Avoid eating before bed:** We tend to make unhealthy eating decisions in the evening. Eating chocolates and snacks in front of the TV tends to be a habit rather than a response to hunger, so it is a good idea to put a blanket ban on eating after your evening meal.

- **Take up a new sport:** Regular exercise has many positive health benefits that help to build your physical resilience. Experiment with a new sport and try to find a form of exercise that you find genuinely fun: This will make it a lot easier to stick to it.

Social Resilience

Meanwhile, your social resilience refers to your interpersonal life. A big part of mental resilience is having a support network when you are feeling troubled. Many men allow their social lives to take a backseat behind family commitments and their work.

Though it's good to support your family, it is also to everyone's benefit that you keep up with your friends. It will give you a chance to let off some steam and relax, which will make you less stressed at work and in your home life. This, in turn, will make you more motivated and productive in those other important aspects of life.

Parceling time for your social life may be more efficient in the long run by helping you be your best at work and with your family. With this in mind, try to schedule some social time at least once a week to keep everything on an even keel.

Spiritual Resilience

Finally, your spiritual resilience is all about your sense of purpose and fulfillment. This doesn't necessarily relate to faith or religion. As an exercise, think about what you believe your purpose is and what your goals are. Having these in mind can help boost your resilience when times are difficult because you will know what you are working toward and struggling for. A sense of purpose—whether it be to provide for your family, to excel in your career, or to honor God—can help you overcome times of trial and suffering. It should not be overlooked.

Techniques for Mindfulness and Self-Awareness

A huge part of Stoicism is self-reflection: looking back on the events of the day and understanding why you acted in the manner that you did. This self-reflection allows you to identify your triggers and your patterns of behavior, empowering you to make better decisions in the future.

We can improve our self-reflection skills by working on our self-awareness. This means working on identifying how we are feeling in a given moment. In turn, this habit is conditioned by practicing mindfulness techniques. Mindfulness helps us stay in the present, focusing our attention on our emotions and physical sensations.

A very simple mindfulness exercise focuses on your breathing, which is also helpful in times of stress or anxiety. It requires no prior experience or expertise and can be done anywhere at any time. This is the 4-7-8 breathing technique, which has only four steps:

1. Inhale slowly through your nose for 4 seconds.

2. Hold your breath for 7 seconds.

3. Exhale slowly through your mouth for 8 seconds.

4. Repeat the first three steps as many times as you like.

Another valuable mindfulness technique is the body scan. This involves focusing on and redirecting your attention to different parts of your body, reflecting on what that body part is feeling.

Through this exercise, you improve your ability to focus your attention; it also helps you stay in the present and relieve anxiety. Follow the steps below to try a body scan for yourself:

1. **Find a comfortable position:** Find a position that's comfortable to you, whether that's sitting down with your back straight and your feet touching the floor or lying down. Try to practice your scan in a place that's quiet and without distractions.

2. **Take a few deep breaths:** You can practice a few cycles of the 4-7-8 breathing technique to help you get into a mindful state.

3. **Bring your attention to your body:** Before starting the scan itself, think about what sensations you can feel: where your body touches other surfaces, what the temperature is, and whether you have any aches or pains. There is no need to evaluate these sensations. Instead, simply note them without judgment.

4. **Begin the body scan:** You can start either at the top of your head and work down or at your toes and work up. For each body part, consider any physical sensations, whether that be physical contact with a surface, pain or aches, or the feeling of that body part against the air.

5. **Remember to keep breathing:** Keep your breathing slow and measured, especially if you identify a pain or ache. You may find it helpful to imagine the pain dissipating with each breath: This can bring pain relief to the affected body part.

6. **Scan your entire body:** Move from body part to body part. Try to stay on each for at least a few seconds so that you can fully identify any physical sensations you're feeling. When you redirect your attention to another part of your body, do so calmly and gently.

If you find your attention drifting, don't get frustrated or upset. Simply note that your attention has drifted, and gently redirect your focus back to the body scan.

You may find it helpful to use a directed body scan, in which you listen to someone who guides you through the exercise. A quick YouTube search will bring up hundreds of guided mindfulness exercises, from body scans to breathing exercises to meditations. Find your favorite and go with what works for you.

Dealing With Stress and Adversity

Mindfulness techniques like those we have already outlined can be very helpful for boosting your mental resilience, which in turn will improve your ability to manage stress and adversity. Remember that dealing with these challenges doesn't involve pretending that your troubles don't exist. Instead, you should try to process your feelings in a healthy, forthright manner, such as by speaking to your partner and friends, taking steps to improve the situation instead of ignoring problems, and practicing self-reflection and mindfulness.

An excellent way of further helping with stress and adversity is to remember what you have to be grateful for. Gratitude exercises can seem a little strange at first, but studies show that practicing gratitude can boost your mental and physical health (Wong et al., 2016). Gratitude exercises can improve your spiritual resilience, remind you what you are struggling to overcome them for, and help put your problems into the proper perspective.

A very simple gratitude exercise only requires a pen and a piece of paper, though it may be worth investing in a journal if you don't have one. At the end of each day, write down one to three things you are grateful for. These can be as detailed or simple as you like. Don't worry if you repeat yourself from day to day. Just make sure that your reflections are genuine and heartfelt. Over time, the act of writing them down will help to internalize your gratitude and keep you optimistic and positive.

Part 2:

Daily Stoicism and Dealing With the World

*Say to yourself first thing in the morning: today I shall meet people who are meddling, ungrateful, aggressive, treacherous, malicious, unsocial. All this has afflicted them through their ignorance of true good and evil. But I have seen that the nature of good is what is right, and the nature of evil what is wrong; and I reflected that the nature of the offender himself is akin to my own—not a kinship of blood or seed, but a sharing in the same mind, the same fragment of divinity. Therefore, I cannot be harmed by any of them, as none will infect me with their wrong. Nor can I be angry with my kinsman or hate him. We were born for co-operation... to work in opposition to one another is against nature. –*Marcus Aurelius

In Part 1, we considered what it is to be a modern Stoic man, looking at the history of Stoicism and how its teachings connect to our lives today. In Part 2, we will think more about the application of Stoic thought and how the philosophy of Stoicism should guide you in your everyday life. This ranges from your daily self-reflections and routines to your conduct at work and in public to your approach to romantic and family relationships.

As we consider how Stoicism connects these common aspects of your everyday life, we will find that three of the tenets of the philosophy are particularly relevant:

- Tenet 1: Live according to nature

- Tenet 3: We cannot control external events, only our opinions, choices, thoughts, and actions

- Tenet 5: Apatheia: eliminate negative emotions and overreactions

As the quotation from Marcus Aurelius above makes clear, the world is full of daily trials that test your patience and temper or tempt you to improper behavior. If anything, the modern world has made such trials utterly ubiquitous. You will be cut off in traffic, treated inconsiderately by your fellow man, and face snideness from your colleagues and bosses. Modern capitalism will tempt you to indulge in overly sugary or salty foods or to buy things you don't need through a constant bombardment of advertisements.

If you are to find eudaemonia and live according to Stoic principles, you will need to show determination and self-control. You will need to live according to your nature as a rational human being. You will need to recognize that you are a reasonable creature who does not act on impulse alone and recognize which actions, foods, and indulgences are appropriate for your body.

You will need to make clear distinctions between what you can control and what you cannot control, demonstrating the wisdom and temperance required to let go of those things that fall beyond your power. Additionally, you will need to exert the self-control necessary to rise above minor annoyances and temptations that will constantly distract you from living a better life.

Finally, you will need to hold true to the four cardinal virtues. Since you cannot control the outside world, you will need to remain calm, objective, and rational in your responses. Nature is rational, but not always in conformity with what you want. You must therefore fit yourself into the world.

Chapter 4:
Daily Exercises to Improve Emotional Readiness to Integrate Stoicism Into Everyday Life

MASTERY OF SELF THROUGH
DAILY PRACTICE

To live according to Stoic principles is like a skill: It requires developing habits, constant reinforcement, and practice. This has two immediate corollaries.

The first corollary is that you do not have to do everything at once. The founder of the school of Stoicism, Zeno, wrote that "well-being is attained by little and little, and nevertheless is no little thing itself" (quoted in Laertius, 2018/3rd Century A.D.). To live the ideal Stoic life is just that—an ideal—and you do not need to beat yourself up if you sometimes fall short. As you keep persevering and practicing, you will get better at living according to Stoic principles and start to reap the benefits of a well-lived life.

The second corollary pushes in the other direction. Though you don't have to do everything at once, the responsibility for your progress lies with you. Like any habit, you must reinforce positive patterns of thought and behavior through hard work and determination. You must demonstrate that you are disciplined and that you have the inner strength to continue when you are tempted to throw in the towel. Even when you do not feel like it, you need to keep practicing and improving.

This chapter outlines daily exercises that tie into both corollaries. On the one hand, they are exercises that help you to practice and improve your ability to live according to Stoic principles, building up your skills one day at a time. On the other hand, you need to practice them regularly, to maintain your sense of discipline, and to internalize the lessons that these exercises impart. Remember that success or failure lies in your hands, and you need to rise to the occasion.

The Principles of a Good Habit

To get the most out of these exercises, you will need to practice them habitually. With this in mind, it is worth taking a little time to outline what makes a good habit, so that you are empowered to succeed.

A good habit has five key aspects. It is:

Specific

A good habit is *specific* in its goals. This helps you to hold yourself accountable to that habit and avoids vagueness that might undermine your motivation. For example, you might decide that every day you want to practice one Stoic exercise in the morning and one in the evening. This is nicely clear and specific, and it's much better than the somewhat vague, "My goal is to do more Stoic exercises."

Bear in mind that a habit can be specific and still changeable. For example, if you get to a point where you think you can do more than two Stoic exercises a day, you can modify your goals accordingly. Specific doesn't mean immutable. It just means that it is not vague.

Measurable

Similarly, a good habit is *measurable*. This might be provided by the specificity of your goals. Continuing the example from the last paragraph, you can measure if you are keeping to your habit very straightforwardly: How many days did you do at least one Stoic exercise in the morning and at least one Stoic exercise in the evening? This allows you to track your progress, and once again hold yourself accountable for meeting your commitment.

Flexible

Next, think about whether your habit is *flexible*. By this, we mostly mean that a good habit is one that is compatible with other commitments in your life. On some occasions, you may not be in a position to complete a Stoic exercise in the evening. Maybe you have to work late, and when you get home, you are in no position to do anything but go to bed and get some sleep.

Recognize from the outset that this is okay. If you like, you can put procedures in place to make up for the missed exercise, such as by planning on completing an extra exercise the next day. Alternatively, you can simply accept that you were not able to complete an evening exercise today and make your peace with that.

The main point behind flexibility is to avoid feeling excessively guilty when you are unable to keep to your habit. Guilt can motivate, but excessive guilt tends to demotivate. Generally, you want to feel good about your habit, rather than resentful toward it. If you start to resent your new habit, you are more likely to abandon it altogether.

Supported

Furthermore, a good habit is *supported*. Continuing the example, it is ideal if you could commit to morning and evening Stoic exercises along with a friend, roommate, or family member. This allows you to motivate one another and hold each other accountable when you are feeling lazy or unenthusiastic. However, if you can't convince someone else to practice the exercises, it is still a great idea to tell someone about your new habit. Simply telling another person about your habit makes it more likely that you'll keep to it because you are now loosely accountable to that person. For maximum benefits, pick someone who is both enthused by your new habit and who is supportive.

Fun

Finally, try to make your new habit *fun*. If you are really not gelling with a particular Stoic exercise, then consider replacing it with another exercise and experimenting with what feels best for you. Additionally, if you need a little extra encouragement, consider linking your Stoic exercises to a small treat like a square of chocolate, or a nice mug of morning coffee. Reward yourself for completing an exercise with that treat, and you'll start to associate the exercise with these positive emotions.

Morning and Evening Routines

Now that we understand that living according to Stoic principles is a habit and that a good habit is specific, measurable, flexible, supported, and fun, it is time to think about some specific Stoic exercises that you might incorporate into your morning and evening routines.

Morning Affirmations

An excellent start to the day is to use an affirmation that relates to Stoic thinking. it is best to say your chosen affirmation aloud so that it is a deliberate and definitive act. Try to choose an affirmation that is personal to you and speaks to what you want to improve upon in how you act and react to life's challenges.

Some Stoic affirmations from ancient Stoic thinkers include:

- "Just that do the right thing. The rest doesn't matter." (Aurelius, 2006/161-180 A.D.)

- "A real man doesn't give way to anger." (Aurelius)

- "Waste no more time arguing what a good man should be. Be one." (Aurelius)

- "It is not events that disturb people, it is their judgments concerning them." (Epictetus, 2008/c.108 A.D.)

- "As each day arises, welcome it as the very best day of all, and make it your own possession. We must seize what flees." (Seneca, 2017/c.65 A.D.)

- "Misfortune is virtue's opportunity." (Seneca)

- "We suffer more in our imagination more often than in reality." (Seneca)

You may also find it useful to make an affirmation of your own. Think about the four cardinal virtues of wisdom, courage, justice, and temperance, and think about where you sometimes fall short. Reflect on your own nature and construct an affirmation that speaks to your personal journey toward a life of Stoic principles.

Voluntary Hardship

Many of the ancient Stoics suffered hardships. Zeno of Citium suffered a disastrous shipwreck. Epictetus was a former slave. Seneca suffered exile and eventual execution. Even Marcus Aurelius, despite his privilege as Roman Emperor, acutely felt the pressures and responsibility of his role.

In addition to these external events, the ancient Stoics also practiced voluntary hardship. Epictetus lived frugally all his life, even when he was freed. Zeno also lived well beneath his means rather than spend his wealth on possessions and food. By practicing humility and undertaking voluntary hardship, the early Stoics built their resilience to the disasters of life. They proved to themselves that they had the inner strength to overcome external events that they could not control.

You might also practice voluntary hardship to build your resilience to external pressures and to practice gratitude for the things that you have. You don't need to give up all your wealth or only eat uncooked food. There are many smaller acts of voluntary hardship that can reinforce your inner strength without you committing yourself to the ascetic life. Some examples include:

- **Taking a cold morning shower:** In addition to building your resilience, taking cold showers in the morning has been linked to improving your metabolism and enhancing circulation (Watson, 2017). They are also an excellent way to quickly wake up in the morning!

- **Having the occasional fast day:** On these days, try not to consume more than 650 calories. This will build resilience and a sense of gratitude toward food and can also help you lose weight and maintain a healthier lifestyle (Torrens, 2023). Just make sure to drink plenty of water on those days so you can remain properly hydrated.

- **Sleeping on the floor occasionally:** You'll soon learn to feel grateful for your bed, and you will prove to yourself that you are made of sterner stuff. Sleeping on the floor may also help your posture and relieve back pain (Nunez, 2019), but make sure you speak to a doctor beforehand if you have pre-existing back issues.

Not all voluntary hardships are physical, however. If you are shy, you might consider putting yourself out there by volunteering to speak at the next meeting at work or else by making a commitment to talk to one stranger a day. This will have the dual benefit of pushing you out of your comfort zone—and proving to yourself that you can confront this fear—as well as improving your interpersonal skills and sense of well-being (Shpancer, 2021).

Committing to One Virtue

The journey to living according to Stoic principles is taken one step at a time. A great way to practice your Stoicism is to start your morning by thinking about how you can demonstrate one of the cardinal virtues in your upcoming day.

Try to be specific. Instead of committing to courage, for example, think about a routine part of your day that either requires courage or else tests it. As in the example above, if you are naturally shy, you might commit to talking to a stranger or striking up a conversation with your coworker. If you have been noticing that an acquaintance keeps getting picked on, you might decide that today's the day you will stand up for them.

At the end of the day, think back on whether you followed through on your commitment. If you did, think about how it made you feel to act virtuously. Reflect on whether it was as difficult as you thought it would be and what you were thinking and feeling before and after. Meanwhile, if you didn't follow through on your commitment, think about why that was and what you might do to have a better chance of success the next day.

Some examples of virtuous actions are included below, but remember to tailor your own commitments to the particulars of your life and experience:

- **Wisdom**

    o Commit to not getting angry on your daily commute by recognizing that the actions of other drivers are beyond your control.

    o Invite the alternative perspective of a colleague or acquaintance on an ongoing project to see things from another point of view.

- **Courage**

    o Tell your rude coworker calmly but firmly that you don't find their put-downs to be appropriate for the workplace.

    o Voice an unpopular opinion you may have about a film or piece of music in your next lunch break, even if it might be unpopular.

- **Justice**

    o Talk to your boss about how one of your quieter colleagues has been essential for the success of your group project to ensure they get the credit.

- o Make amends for a time you were rude or selfish to a friend, either by apologizing or otherwise making an effort to make it right.

- **Temperance**

  - o Avoid snacking mindlessly throughout the day and only eat your prepared meals.

  - o Commit to responding with a smile or a compliment the first time someone is rude to you.

Self-Reflections

In addition to some morning and evening routines, it is worth thinking about the role self-reflection plays in a Stoic life.

As we've noted in earlier chapters, the Stoics strongly believed in the importance of self-reflection. Because they realized that we cannot control external events, they knew that it was important to have an understanding of those elements of life that we can control: our own actions and thoughts.

Self-reflection helps you understand yourself so that you can improve and live more virtuously. It also helps in identifying pitfalls and barriers to living a more fulfilling life. In addition, it is a way of holding yourself accountable and demonstrating radical honesty with yourself.

With this in mind, try to complete at least one self-reflection exercise a day. One example of such an exercise is to practice gratitude, which we outlined at the end of Chapter 3. In this chapter, we outline another three self-reflection exercises that can help you practice and perfect your Stoic mindset.

Cognitive Behavioral Therapy and Self-Reflection

Many Stoic teachings can be found in modern psychology and therapy, demonstrating the wisdom and influence of these ancient ideas. In particular, the idea of examining your own patterns of thought and behavior is utilized in cognitive behavioral therapy (CBT). These updated ancient ideas can be powerful means of improving your well-being and improving your ability to live according to Stoic principles.

At the heart of CBT is something called the cognitive cycle. The idea behind this is that our thoughts, behaviors, physical sensations, and emotions are all mutually interconnected and have a causal effect on each other. To give a simple example, if you are hungry (a physical sensation), you are likely to be irritable (an emotion), to snap at your colleagues (a behavior), and to ruminate about all the things that annoy you (a thought).

The point is that these four facets influence each other in all directions. To continue the example, ruminating about all the things that annoy you is likely to make you feel more irritable, which will make you more likely to snap at a colleague. Feeling irritable (an emotion) is likely to raise your body temperature (a physical sensation). And so on.

The key idea behind CBT is that it is much easier to influence your thoughts and behaviors than it is to directly change how you feel. Moreover, because of the cognitive cycle, you can affect how you feel by putting into place more positive thought and behavior patterns. By recognizing how negative behavior patterns feed into feelings of anxiety, for example, you can alleviate your symptoms of anxiety by replacing those negative patterns of behavior with more positive alternatives.

This brings us back to self-reflection and Stoicism. An excellent self-reflection exercise is to think about the last time you felt angry, sad, or otherwise upset and to consider what you were thinking or how you were behaving when you felt that way. By writing down these self-reflections, you can then begin to look over your past reflections and start to identify patterns. This, in turn, will pinpoint places where you can make improvements.

Let's consider this in a specific example. Suppose you felt guilty at some point today. You reflect on this incident and consider the thoughts and behaviors that surrounded this event. In this case, you felt guilty when you snacked on donuts during work. The behavior is very clear: It was the act of eating a donut.

Continue your reflections and go a little deeper. Think about the physical sensations you were feeling. Were you hungry? What had you been doing just before the event: Were you working on a difficult problem or completing an unpleasant task? And what were you thinking before and after? Were you bargaining with yourself? Were you berating yourself? Did your inner monologue sound like anyone else you know, such as one of your parents, or an old bully?

As you complete these self-reflections and then review them in your journal, you'll start to identify patterns that in turn suggest areas for improvement. Maybe you always snack around the time that you are doing your least favorite bit of work. An immediate solution might be to rearrange your day, so you take on that task after lunch when you are most satiated and least likely to snack.

Maybe you start to realize that your thoughts are very self-critical, such that you can consciously work on replacing that inner voice with one that is more compassionate toward yourself. Over time, you will understand your nature more clearly and thus be able to help yourself overcome the trials and tribulations of daily life.

Negative Visualizations

Negative visualization requires you to consciously reflect on unpleasant events that might occur. If you are feeling worried about a project at work, you might visualize what would happen should the project go entirely wrong. If you are feeling anxious about an upcoming date, you might visualize the worst possible scenario, like imagining your date sneaking out and ditching you, or you two not having much of an emotional connection.

Negative visualization is a form of self-reflection that helps you prepare for the worst. It serves multiple purposes. First, it is a kind of rehearsal. When you practice negative visualizations, you should think about how you would react and reflect on the most virtuous way to behave in those instances. Should these negative events then take place, you will already be prepared to react virtuously. You will be empowered to be the best version of yourself in those moments.

Second, negative visualization can be comforting. By imagining the worst-case scenario, you might come to the realization that it wouldn't really be so bad. A bad date isn't going to ruin your life. A failed project at work won't result in any lasting consequences other than a bit of sternness from your boss. By imagining these negative events and reflecting on how they are unlikely to be life-changing, you can feel a little calmer about those worries that are bothering you. You build your resilience and achieve more control over how you will react and feel.

Finally, negative visualizations are a form of voluntary hardship. It can be uncomfortable to think about events going wrong, especially if they connect to matters that are important to you. By putting yourself in that mindset, you can strengthen your inner resilience, providing yourself with a little bit of exposure therapy for those things you are worried about.

A very famous version of negative visualization is encapsulated in the phrase *memento mori*: a Latin phrase that translates to "remember you must die." It is said that a successful Roman general would return home to victory parades, but a slave would constantly follow and murmur the phrase in his ear. The idea was to keep the general grounded and humble despite his glories so that he would not think himself a god.

Reflecting on death is a Stoic tradition. Thinking about death can help remove some of the fear surrounding it, which empowers you to act in a manner that is courageous and virtuous. Furthermore, reflecting on death is motivating. As Seneca wrote, "It is not that we have a short time to live but that we waste a lot of it" (Seneca, 2017/c.65 A.D.).

Marcus Aurelius was even more direct: "You could leave life right now. Let that determine what you do and say and think" (Aurelius, 2006/161-180 A.D.).

The View From Above

The final self-reflection we'll consider in this chapter is the "view from above" exercise. The idea behind this exercise is to give yourself a sense of perspective, which will not only keep you humble but will make it easier to tolerate the hardships of life. You will recognize that your problems are not as great as you perceive them to be, which will give you the perspective you need to persevere and thrive.

You can search for "the view from above" on YouTube and find guided meditations that take you through this self-reflection. Alternatively, you can practice the exercise by yourself by following beautifully explained directions from the famous advocate of Stoicism, Ryan Holiday (n.d.):

I recommend going somewhere relaxing, such as a park or the beach if you're lucky enough to live in a coastal area. Obviously, I can't tell you exactly what to imagine because I'm not you, but I would recommend starting above the clouds and then slowly come closer to the world and the people in it. Feel free to start much, much farther away in some distant spot of the universe. Observe everything going on: first kisses, wars, discoveries, learning, artistic creations, traffic jams, and anything else you can imagine. Observe, but do not judge. Now think of yourself in relation to all of this. Know, that many of the things you hold to be important are only relatively important. Know that *you* are only relatively important. (para 14)

Chapter 5:

Managing Work Issues Stoically

WITH WISDOM AT WORK, IN HARMONY WITH ALL.

In this chapter, we focus more on bringing a Stoic mindset to the workplace.

As we have already discussed in previous chapters, there are many ways in which the workplace can test your virtuousness. Petty annoyances like irritating coworkers, IT issues, and micromanaging bosses can make it difficult to keep your cool and act in a way that is temperate and wise. Your work may be stressful, or you may witness bullying in the workplace that calls for your courage and innate sense of justice.

However, remember that every hardship is an opportunity to practice virtue. By taking these opportunities as they come, you can rise to the occasion and continue to flourish.

Leadership, Ethics, and Success

Many of the ancient Stoics were themselves leaders of men. Marcus Aurelius, as Roman Emperor, was one of the most powerful men in the ancient world. Seneca was a Roman senator, and Zeno founded an entire school of philosophy. This pedigree speaks to another advantage of the Stoic life: The lessons of Stoicism are highly applicable to leadership.

Even if you are not yourself a manager, you have opportunities to show leadership in group projects and in your personal conduct. This doesn't mean that you should steamroll over everyone else. It just means that you should show leadership in how you conduct your affairs and act to help others remain motivated and productive.

When it comes to leadership, one very important lesson of Stoicism is the third tenet: recognizing the difference between what you can control and what you cannot. One of the cardinal sins of bad managers is the need to micromanage. Such managers spread themselves too thin by trying to control everything, even those external events that are beyond their power. Not only is this a waste of energy and productive time, but it is also highly irritating to those who are being hovered over. Constantly having to explain yourself to your manager can be demotivating and also costs time that you could otherwise be spending on your work itself.

With this in mind, if you are in a position of leadership, make peace with the fact that you are not going to be able to control everything. Show your wisdom by delegating and your courage by putting your trust in your coworkers and those working under you.

54

A good manager is someone who can keep their cool and maintain apatheia, as per the fifth tenet of Stoicism. By practicing Stoic exercises and working on your temperance, you will be able to put minor roadblocks and problems into their proper perspective. You will have the wisdom to see that some external events are beyond the control of you and your team. Instead, you will be able to spend your efforts on bringing practical solutions to problems rather than being overwhelmed by them.

For example, suppose that there is a workflow blockage: You are waiting on a report from another team before your own work can progress. The delay from the other team threatens to put you behind schedule. It would be natural to feel irritable or stressed or to complain bitterly about the other team. However, this is unproductive and intemperate. Instead, think about how you can apply the tenets of Stoicism to this situation.

First, you might show wisdom by considering what lies within your control. You can't control the fact that there have already been delays, but you might have some influence on whether the delays continue. You could speak to the manager of the other team—calmly and politely—and ask for an update on their schedule while explaining the time pressures on your own projects. This is a productive and proactive step you can take, demonstrating real leadership in a difficult situation.

Second, you could apply Stoic thinking to recognize that this is not a huge problem in the greater scheme of things. For example, you might use the view-from-above reflection (outlined at the end of Chapter 4) to shift your perspective. There are many more important things happening than a delay of a few days.

You might reflect on the fact that this is not a problem that will upset you next month or maybe even next week. By putting the problem in its proper perspective, you can maintain your temperance and keep calm. This will allow you to remain proactive and productive rather than being overwhelmed with stress. For example, you might reorganize your project so that work can continue while you are waiting for the other team's report. By reacting calmly and sensibly, you will show leadership to your colleagues. Taking your example, they will be able to remain calm and collected as well.

In addition to helping, you maintain a sense of calmness at work, practicing Stoicism can also help you demonstrate ethical leadership. Glenn Llopis, author of *Leadership in the Age of Personalization*, writes that "the most important ingredient to great management is this: *accountability*" (Llopis, 2012). Stoicism is all about personal accountability. By reflecting on your own behavior each day, you will be able to identify places for improvement as well as steps you can take to correct a mistake.

By being committed to justice, you will accept your errors rather than blaming your team. You will demonstrate to your colleagues that it is alright to make a mistake as long as you take accountability and are proactive in bringing solutions. This will make you a great leader because you will foster an atmosphere of mutual trust, co-operation, and honesty. Your team will trust you to be fair with them, and, in return, they will be fair with you.

Navigating Workplace Challenges

Stubborn coworkers. Delays. Difficult customers. When it comes down to it, all workplace challenges amount to the same thing: stress.

Stoicism has a complex relationship with stress. This is because the Stoics realized that stress can be positive as well as negative. Marcus Aurelius wrote that "a blazing fire makes flame and brightness out of everything that is thrown into it" (Aurelius, 2006/161-180 A.D.). Seneca had a similar view: "Fire is the test of gold; adversity, of strong men" (Seneca, 2017/c.65 A.D.). The point is that stress and hardship are opportunities for personal growth, for virtue, and to prove your inner worth.

Modern psychology confirms that some stress can be a good thing. The Yerkes–Dodson Law holds that the relationship between stress and productivity is a bell curve: A moderate amount of stress can boost productivity but too much can overwhelm you (Nickerson, 2023). With this in mind, let's consider how you can manage stress effectively so that it motivates rather than paralyzes you.

The key is temperance: All things in moderation. This is achieved through self-reflection, courage, and the wisdom to recognize what you can handle. Self-reflection is useful for handling stress because it helps you identify what your stressors are. In Chapter 4, we discussed how self-reflection can identify triggers by finding patterns in habits of thought and behavior. You can apply this same exercise to workplace stress.

Think about the last time you felt so stressed at work that it negatively affected your productivity. For example, perhaps you were working on a difficult problem and, to avoid it, you began procrastinating. This is a classic case of stress undermining your work ethic.

Now think about the behaviors and thoughts that surrounded this incident as well as how you felt both physically and emotionally. You might have had self-critical thoughts and berated yourself for not being smart enough to solve the problem. You might have had a headache; you might have felt tired. Think about when the event happened—maybe it was a few hours after lunch. Try to identify what factors contributed to the stress getting to you and think about what you could have done differently to manage that stress. Taking some of these factors into consideration might provide you with helpful strategies for keeping stress at a productive level.

To take an example, suppose you tend to get stressed a few hours after lunch. If you have a tendency to eat a little unhealthily, this might be due to an insulin crash. You ate sugary foods, leading to an insulin spike, which then led to a crash after an hour or so. This can make you feel irritable and stressed. A future solution therefore presents itself. In the future, you might cut down on sugary foods and choose meals with more protein and whole grains.

This is just one example. The point is that you should take steps to understand your stressors and understand what makes you tick so that you can apply that understanding and improve your well-being. Approach yourself with curiosity, like a scientist, and utilize any nuggets of wisdom you find.

Similarly, you can manage your stress by adopting a proper sense of perspective. Remember that you might not get to control the overall situation but that you are a rational being who gets to control how they react and behave. Remember also that the world is very big, and you occupy a relatively small part of it. No workplace problem is worth losing your head over, so live according to your nature and respond with calmness and reason.

On the other side, you can think about how Stoicism relates to workplace challenges and embracing stress. By committing yourself to virtuous action, you will know not to shy away from difficulty and hardship but instead to embrace challenges where they come.

Your self-reflections can give you strategies for helping you manage stress, but you also need to bring some grit and determination to hardship. Think about how you can rise to the occasion and prove your inner strength in those moments of difficulty.

Remain disciplined in the face of stress. Reflect on how you have met similar challenges in the past to prove to yourself that you have what it takes to meet and overcome the current obstacle. Every difficulty and hardship are an opportunity for you to prove your virtuousness and strength.

Finally, remember Epictetus's words (2008/c.108 A.D.):

What would have become of Hercules, do you think, if there had been no lion, hydra, stag, or boar—and no savage criminals to rid the world of? What would he have done in the absence of such challenges? Obviously, he would have just rolled over in bed and gone back to sleep. So, by snoring his life away in luxury and comfort he never would have developed into the mighty Hercules.

Your workplace problems might not involve lions or hydras, but they are challenges that shape your character and make you a better man. As such, welcome the challenge and prove yourself against it.

Integrity and Collaboration

Just as challenges make a man, conflict in the workplace is not necessarily a bad thing. Conflicting opinions can give rise to new ideas, help you see problems from a different point of view, and provide opportunities to work on your interpersonal skills.

However, this doesn't mean that you should foster conflict unnecessarily or allow workplace conflicts to become heated or personal. Remember the virtue of temperance, and don't contribute to a situation that is more about emotion than reason. Your goal should first and foremost be about problem-solving and co-operation rather than boosting personal egos.

This means acting virtuously even in instances of conflict. Show wisdom and humility in properly listening to other points of view and have the courage to allow your opinions to be challenged without getting defensive. Furthermore, show your commitment to justice by making sure everyone has the chance to say their piece. Similarly with temperance, by remaining patient and empathetic to everyone at the table. If you think you have made a mistake, demonstrate your integrity to others and admit that it is so. We are often afraid of admitting error as if it will make us look weak, but, in reality, only people who are insecure about their intelligence or competence are unable to admit when they have made a mistake. People respect men who hold themselves to account and who understand their limits.

On the other hand, Stoicism doesn't ask you to be a pushover. Listen honestly to other opinions, but if you think you are right, stand by your beliefs. Don't compromise just for the sake of avoiding conflict: Instead, you should only compromise if such an action would be wise or just. In particular, show courage and conviction on matters of morality and stand up for what you believe.

Confrontation can feel unpleasant, but it is just another opportunity for virtue. Like all hardships, it will pass, and what will stay with you is not the confrontation itself, but how you acted and defended your beliefs.

Do you want to look back and see someone who was weak and cowardly? Or do you want to look back and see someone with conviction and integrity?

The key, then, is finding balance. Sticking to your principles is well and good, but if you are digging your heels in over relatively minor matters, then you run the risk of simply being stubborn and bullheaded. You should be honest with yourself and resist the lure of ego. If you are defending your position simply for the sake of not backing down, you are being vain. By contrast, if you are defending your position because it is morally right, you should have the courage to do so.

A particular type of workplace conflict worth talking about is bullying. The 2021 WBI U.S. Workplace Bullying Survey (Namie, 2021) found that more than 13% of American adults have experienced bullying in the last year, amounting to some 21 million people.

If you are personally being bullied, then you can use Stoic teaching to better handle the situation. You may not be able to control whether a colleague is rude or snide to you, but you have control over how you respond and feel about the situation. Often, bullying peters out when it is obvious that the person being bullied won't rise to the provocation. If you are being insulted, live according to your nature, decide on how you want to react, and show your bully that their words do not harm you.

Depending on the level of bullying, however, you may want to apply Stoic principles to stand up for yourself. It can take courage to set boundaries, especially if your bully doesn't realize that they are doing something wrong. It can feel awkward and uncomfortable. However, it is important to show courage and correct the situation with calmness and firmness. Speak to the individual in private about how their behavior is unacceptable and don't rise to provocation or baiting. Show your strength.

Finally, if you see someone else being bullied, stand up for them. People often mistake Stoicism for apathy or tolerating abuse, but in truth, there is no justice or courage in standing by when someone is being picked on. Extend compassion to the victim, stand beside them, and tell the bully that what they are doing is wrong. It may be difficult and stressful, but you will go to sleep that night knowing that you are a man of integrity and strength.

Chapter 6:
Relationships and Stoicism

Just as living in accordance with the teachings of Stoicism can help you navigate challenges at work, adopting a Stoic mindset can help you in your personal relationships. In this chapter, we will think about relationships and Stoicism and consider how the ideal Stoic conducts himself toward those he cares about.

We will mostly focus on romantic relationships, but many of the lessons are equally applicable to other important relationships in your life, such as close friendships and family ties. The basic principles of acting with integrity, virtue, and not attempting to control what you cannot are all highly useful for navigating personal relationships and adopting a healthy approach to your interpersonal life.

As we have mentioned earlier in this book, Stoicism is often misunderstood as a heartless philosophy. According to this misconception, some might think that a Stoic man is incapable of love. But this, of course, is just a mistaken belief. Though Stoicism teaches that it is manly to be in control of your emotions, that doesn't mean that you have to deny them entirely. It just means that intense emotions like jealousy and lust aren't allowed to override your natural reason and lead you to make bad decisions.

Building Meaningful Connections

Through its focus on integrity and virtue, Stoicism asks us to be honest in our dealings with other people—and honesty is a very important aspect of a meaningful relationship.

Dr. Sabrina Romanoff, a Harvard-trained clinical psychologist, outlines the importance of honesty in a romantic relationship (quoted in Gupta, 2023):

Honesty in a romantic relationship is about being authentic and genuine with your partner. It requires saying what you feel and think without hiding, suppressing, or manipulating your words. (para 4)

Stoicism helps you be honest in your relationships by encouraging you to be courageous in expressing your feelings and temperate in how you communicate your needs. It also advocates the self-reflection and wisdom necessary to understand your own feelings so that you can communicate them with clarity in a constructive manner.

Think about your Stoicism exercises and how they might be applied to your relationships. Self-reflection exercises can help you identify patterns of thought and behavior that cause problems in your relationship, allowing you to discuss them with your partner. Reflection exercises such as the view from above help you get a proper perspective so that you can avoid getting too worked up about minor irritations like your partner leaving hairs in the sink or shirking on their fair share of chores.

Gratitude exercises can further help you find a sense of perspective so that you don't risk blowing up a good thing on the basis of some small quibbles that can be reasonably discussed. Mindfulness and stress-relief techniques can help ground you in the present and let go of historical grievances while helping you keep your cool in the moment.

Furthermore, Stoicism has lessons for us when it comes to establishing meaningful relationships or else letting go when the romantic connection you hoped for is not going to happen. In particular, the ancient Stoics warned against getting caught up in unrequited love. Remember the third tenet of Stoicism—that it is important to recognize the difference between what you can control and what you cannot. A big aspect of life you can't control is whether other people find you attractive.

Of course, there are some elements that fall within your control. If you are a little overweight and this is affecting your self-confidence in potential partners finding you physically attractive, you can work on getting into shape. If your short temper or lack of confidence is preventing you from getting a second date, you can work on managing your emotions more effectively. Ultimately, though, there is going to be a limit to what you can control.

We all have our preferences when it comes to potential romantic partners, and the fact is that you are not going to be all things to all people. You simply cannot change that. Such situations can be painful but remember: This too shall pass. Use exercises that help you find a fresh perspective and recognize that whatever it is that is bothering you about your relationship or finding a romantic partner is something that you will feel differently about in the future. For example, a particularly useful exercise requires thinking about how you are likely to feel about the situation at a later point:

1. Write down the situation and how it makes you feel. Try to understand your own nature when you do this.

2. Now, write down how you are likely to feel about the situation in one month, taking note of any changes you predict.

3. Next, write down how you are likely to feel about the situation in one year, taking note of any anticipated changes.

4. Finally, write down how you are likely to feel about the situation in ten years, taking note of any changes you expect.

When it comes to an unrequited crush, it is unlikely that you'll even remember the situation 10 years from now. If you meet someone in the meantime, you might not think about it after one year—at the very least, it is unlikely to trouble you in the slightest. And, unless you're crushing very hard, it is pretty likely that you'll feel much better about it after just a month. In short: You'll feel better if you allow yourself a bit of time.

On the other hand, if you do make a romantic connection with someone, remember that all things end one way or another: Memento mori. This doesn't mean that you have to be gloomy and pessimistic, but it does mean that you should value what you have in the moment you have it and not take it for granted. Brenda Conlon from Medium (2022) references Epictetus's teachings: "We have an allotted time for love, be it six months, six years, or sixty. With that said, Epictetus taught not to be consumed by the love you have for this person but to work on yourself to be the best companion you can be for your partner."

Practicing negative visualizations can also help you prepare for the worst while being open to being the best partner you can be in the present. All relationships end, either with a breakup or a death, and both are likely to be painful. However, by preparing yourself for that eventuality, you can prepare yourself to react in a manner that is virtuous and manly.

If you are a younger man, the chances are that your current or next relationship will end with a breakup. Think about how that's likely to go down. If you identify some problems that might lead to the relationship's end, consider addressing them now rather than allowing them to escalate into something you can no longer control. Be proactive in improving your relationship. However, some relationships just end: The spark fizzles out, or you realize you and your partner want different things from life. That's okay.

Visualize how the relationship might end and how you would like to act in that instance. Prepare yourself to act with compassion and kindness rather than lashing out or losing your temper. Prepare yourself to act like a man rather than a screaming child. That way, if and when the moment comes, you will remain reasonable and virtuous.

Finally, let's talk about lust. The Stoics recognized that sexual desire is a natural part of romantic relationships but warned about letting intemperate emotions in place of reason guide us. This means that you shouldn't let lust override your rational thought. Remember that, though you cannot control whether or not someone is attractive to you, you do get to control how you react to that fact. Finding someone attractive is fine, but you are not an animal. You are a man with reason, and it is worth defending that with self-discipline and temperance.

The ancient Stoics had a technique for helping themselves overcome temptation known as recontextualization. This involves redescribing the focus of your attractions—whether that be sex, a cigarette, or an indulgent chocolate cake—in a manner that is entirely objective. By breaking things down into their basic components, much of the allure can be done away with, allowing you to remain impartial and clearheaded. For example, Marcus Aurelius (2006/161-180 A.D.) described sex as follows: "Friction of the genitals with the excretion of mucus in spasms." Hardly the most alluring picture!

Communication and Empathy

We have touched on how Stoicism advocates honest communication with your partner. It asks you to have the courage to talk about your feelings, the wisdom to identify problems before they become bigger problems than they have to be, and the temperance to talk about your concerns without losing your temper or throwing around accusations. Finally, Stoicism encourages you to show justice in recognizing when you might be in the wrong and in listening properly to your partner's opinions.

Let's think more about this last point. We have focused on how you might express your feelings with honesty, calmness, and integrity, but an important part of communication is also listening. Zeno was quoted by Laertius (2018/3rd century A.D.) as saying, "We have two ears and one mouth therefore we should listen twice as much as we speak." In addition to this wisdom, however, it is important to learn how to listen *well*.

Active Listening

Active listening is an important tool for people with great interpersonal skills, and like any skill, it can be honed and improved with practice. The difference between active and passive listening is the difference between engaging with what the other person said and simply hearing what they have said. It is showing the other person that you are paying attention and processing their words rather than being a recording device. This is an essentially Stoic practice because it is treating other people as what they are: fellow rational beings with something important to say.

Because active listening is such a big part of interpersonal communication, you could write a whole book on the subject. Indeed, many people have. Rather than go into too much detail here, let's consider a few key elements of active listening that you can work on implementing into your daily life:

Body Language

When someone is talking to you, it is important to show that you are listening to them by using your facial expressions and body language. To show interest, think about leaning slightly toward the person you are speaking with, keeping good eye contact, and using the occasional eyebrow flash.

Additionally, your body language should be appropriate for the content of what they're saying. For example, if someone is telling a sad story, or opening up about a painful event, your facial expressions should reflect sympathy and compassion. Imagine telling someone that your cat just died and seeing a huge smile on their face: It would be quite off-putting!

Follow-up Questions

When active listening, you shouldn't be utterly silent. Asking follow-up questions that are pertinent to what the other person is talking about is a great way of showing that you are engaged in the conversation. For example, if someone is telling a story about their lake house, you might ask about how long they've had it or whether they have any recommendations for good fishing spots.

Again, it is worth making sure that your follow-up questions match the tone of the current conversation. Furthermore, it is good not to interrupt, so always take a couple of beats before asking a question. This will ensure that the other person has finished what they were saying rather than just taking a breath.

Paralanguage

In addition to follow-up questions, you can use paralanguage to prompt the other person to keep talking. By "paralanguage," we mean utterances like "uh huh," or "hm." These are the kinds of utterances that are not words but sounds that show you are listening. Being greeted by complete silence can be quite off-putting for the person you are talking to, so try to avoid it.

Paraphrasing

Another excellent way to show you are listening is to paraphrase what the other person has just said. The trick is to know the difference between paraphrasing and parroting. You don't want to simply repeat them, so make sure you rephrase what they've said in your own words and keep it brief.

For example, if the person you are talking to has just finished complaining about their boss, you might paraphrase with, "It sounds like you are getting really frustrated with them." This rephrases rather than simply repeats what they said and also demonstrates empathy by connecting with their emotions.

Ultimately, good listening requires you to foster a genuine curiosity about what the other person has to say. Remember what Epictetus (2008/c.108 A.D.) wrote: "It is impossible for a man to learn what he thinks he always knows." Be open to the idea that the other person might offer a new, interesting perspective, give them the benefit of the doubt, and you will be more enthusiastic and engaged when listening to them.

Being a good communicator is virtuous because it does justice not only to your opinion but to your partner's opinion. By fostering a relationship based on mutual respect, integrity, and trust, you are more likely to build a meaningful and happy relationship. However, in addition to a sense of justice, such a relationship can require courage. As men, we have sometimes been encouraged to repress our feelings or to respond to difficult emotions with anger and irritation. This conception of manliness is outdated, and it certainly isn't Stoic. We must live in accordance with our nature as rational human beings who have emotions. Take that leap of faith with your partner, open up, and enjoy the benefits to your relationship that this will bring.

Conflict Resolution

In Chapter 5, we talked about how conflict isn't necessarily something to be afraid of. If two people in a relationship have a difference of opinion, it is healthier to talk about it and resolve the issue than to let it fester and go unsaid.

Many of the tips for conflict resolution outlined in Chapter 5 apply equally to conflicts in personal relationships. You should aim to act virtuously and to give justice to your view and the perspective of your partner. You should also have the integrity to admit when you are wrong and the courage to stand up for yourself when you are right. Additionally, you should have the wisdom and temperance to outline your position in a way that doesn't bait your partner or else escalate the issue into something that is more disastrous than it has to be.

However, when it comes to conflict in a relationship, the issue at hand can often disguise a more important underlying matter. If your relationship is built on openness and mutual trust, much of this can be avoided. However, the fact is that many people try to overlook problems or grievances for the sake of avoiding confrontation. This can seem reasonable, but if the problems start building up, they'll eventually be expressed in an angry or overly emotional way. If this happens, your job is to remain calm and de-escalate the situation so it can be reasonably and productively discussed.

This requires temperance. It is natural to respond to anger with anger, and if you are the one who has been bottling up frustration with minor problems, it might require powerful self-discipline to climb down from the heightened emotional state you have put yourself in. Take a few deep breaths using the 4-7-8 method, remember that you control how you act and behave, and give yourself permission to calm down. Meanwhile, if the anger is coming from your partner, don't respond in kind. That will simply escalate the situation and make it impossible to reach a sensible resolution to your conflict.

When things have calmed down, it is time to employ wisdom. Try to comprehend the real root of the problem. Ask questions that demonstrate you are genuinely trying to understand. Be open to the idea that there may be something going on that you don't know about. If your partner is exploding at you because you didn't take out the bins, chances are that the real issue isn't just the trash. It might be that it reflects frustration with a pattern of you not helping around the house or otherwise taking your partner for granted. Take the time to fully understand your partner's point of view so you can address their needs directly and forthrightly.

That doesn't mean you have to be a pushover. In fact, Stoicism asks you not to be. Show courage and stand up for yourself if your partner is being unreasonable or bullying you. Continuing the above example: Maybe your partner is blowing up at you over the bins because they've had a bad day and need someone to take it out on. Though this is something people often do and not worth condemning your partner over, it is also not fair to you, and neither is it acceptable. Pointing that out—without raising your voice or losing your temper—is more than reasonable.

On the other hand, if you are at fault, be committed to justice and admit it. Don't keep arguing for the sake of not backing down. That's just fighting for the sake of ego, which is intemperate and unmanly. If there is something you need to make amends for, take proactive steps to do so. Conduct yourself with integrity and show your partner that you can take accountability. That way, when you do stand your ground, your partner will know that you are coming from a position of honesty and honor. Ultimately, remain committed to your principles and sense of what is right.

Integrity

Before we end this chapter, it is worth a brief discussion about integrity that doesn't necessarily involve conflict or romantic relationships. In this section, we'll talk about how you need to take steps to guard your integrity and to be careful with the kind of company you keep.

The ancient Stoics warned that keeping the wrong company can be harmful to your sense of morality. Epictetus (2008/c.108 A.D.) wrote, "If a companion is dirty, his friends cannot help but get a little dirty too, no matter how clean they started out." This idea is also supported by modern psychology. A toxic friend can affect your physical health by increasing the levels of stress proteins that are in the body, resulting in inflammation and other related complications such as depression (Slavich & Irwin, 2014). Toxic relationships can therefore affect both the mind and soul.

When it comes to integrity and morality, the danger presented is bad behavior being normalized by bad company. If your friends are constantly complaining and gossiping, then you might find yourself doing the same thing just to fit in, sometimes without even realizing it. The human tendency to mirror the behavior of other humans is an evolutionary impulse. However, if it comes at the cost of your integrity and sense of moral value, it is worth resisting.

Remember that you always have a choice. Call out bad behavior where you see it and try to influence your friends to conduct themselves better. If that doesn't work, though, it is also important to recognize what you can control and what you cannot. You might not be able to change the behavior of your friends, but you can seek out better company.

Epictetus advised that you should seek out the company of philosophers. As Jonny Thomson from Big Think notes, this doesn't mean that you should only make friends with academics. Remember that, in Epictetus's day, a philosopher was a person concerned with understanding how best to live; they are those "who want to become wiser, kinder, and more fulfilled. They are the ones who make you feel proud about who you are but also who impel you to behave better. They cultivate virtue" (Thomson, 2021).

Find people in your life who cultivate virtue and you will flourish as a result.

Part 3:

Personal Growth

Putting things off is the biggest waste of life: It snatches away each day as it comes, and denies us the present by promising the future. The greatest obstacle to living is expectancy, which hangs upon tomorrow and loses today. You are arranging what lies in Fortune's control, and abandoning what lies in yours. What are you looking at? To what goal are you straining? The whole future lies in uncertainty: Live immediately. –Seneca

If you are reading this book, you are likely dissatisfied with some aspect of your life. You are looking for a philosophy that will help you be a better man and live a better life. The good news is that Stoicism does provide the answers. The bad news is that knowing the answers is not a substitute for hard work.

Stoicism shows you how to live virtuously and with integrity, but it also asks you to persevere and remain disciplined. The brain is trained through habit and repetition. Living virtuously will get easier over time, as will resisting temptation. If you have previously lived in a way that allowed your emotions to rule the roost, it will take time to dislodge those habitual patterns of behavior. You will have to work on them deliberately and with courage, but you will begin to notice improvements over time.

In Part 3 of this book, we look at three topics related to personal growth. We will consider how to set and meet appropriate goals for yourself, aspects of health and fitness, and the importance of embracing your innate creativity. Throughout, we will continue to keep in mind the four cardinal virtues of wisdom, courage, justice, and temperance, and they can be practically applied in your life. We will also emphasize three particular tenets of Stoicism:

- Tenet 2: Fulfilment is not found in things but in actions and virtuous living

- Tenet 4: We have the tools to thrive

- Tenet 9: Progress, not perfection

No matter your start in the world or current situation, you have the power to live a virtuous and more fulfilling life. Because fulfillment comes from action and virtuous living, and you are always in control of how you act, eudaemonia is available to anyone.

However, as we have repeatedly stressed throughout this book, remember that the ideal Stoic life is called "ideal" for a reason. We are not perfect. Marcus Aurelius, one of the most famous Stoics of antiquity, constantly berated himself in his *Meditations* for feeling demotivated or irritable.

If the Roman Emperor Marcus Aurelius can fall short every now and again, so can we. The important thing is to try and be a better man, one day at a time.

Chapter 7:

The Path to Self-Improvement

When thinking about becoming a better man, it is important for you to do so in a directed and goal-orientated way. In Chapter 4, we talked about the hallmarks of a good habit and how the goal of such a habit should be specific and measurable. You should try to keep this in mind, and we will expand on these ideas, but it is also worth thinking about goals that incorporate the lessons and wisdom of Stoicism.

In this chapter, we will think about what kind of goals are appropriate for someone living in accordance with Stoic principles and how you should approach meeting those goals. We will discuss likely obstacles you might run into and how best to overcome them. Furthermore, we will consider what growth might look like and what you should expect from your personal journey to self-improvement. Finally, at the end of the chapter, we will include a template for goal-setting that should help you get started on the right path.

Aligning Goals With Stoic Principles

Modern psychology teaches us that the best goals are SMART (Stibich, 2020):

- **Specific:** As discussed in Chapter 4, a good goal should not be vague. For example, suppose you wanted to get in shape. A vague goal might be to "lose some weight." Instead, you want to choose something specific, such as committing to exercising at least four times a week and losing 10 pounds. Better still, set the times and days you will exercise.

- **Measurable:** By measuring your progress, you are more likely to remain motivated and disciplined. For example, if your goal is to get in shape, then you might set an objective of exercising at least four times a week. By investing in a weekly calendar, you can physically tick off your progress each time you work out.

- **Attainable:** A good goal is realistic. There is nothing more demotivating than a goal that is impossible to reach. Remember that as Stoics, we are concerned with progress, not perfection. Continuing the example of getting in shape, your goal should be to lose 10 pounds (keeping things nice and specific), not to become an Olympic athlete in 2 months.

- **Relevant:** Your goal should be relevant to your personal ambitions and tailored to you. It makes no sense to set a goal that isn't important to you as you are unlikely to care about meeting it. Moreover, it is important to choose methods of meeting your aims that suit your lifestyle and preferences. If your goal is to get in shape, then choose a form of exercise that you actually enjoy rather than something you hate.

- **Time-bound:** By making your goal time-bound, you set an expectation by which you can hold yourself to account. Continuing with our example, you might decide to exercise four times a week for the next 10 weeks. At the end of the 10 weeks, you can congratulate yourself and reassess what the next goal on your health journey should be.

The important thing about SMART goals is that they keep you accountable. This means that these aspects—objectives being specific, measurable, attainable, relevant, and time-bound—align well with Stoic principles. Stoicism is about holding yourself responsible and identifying areas for self-improvement. The fundamental Stoic principles of honesty and integrity mesh well with SMART goals because they help you identify where you are succeeding or falling short in a straightforward way.

They also help you implement strategies to ensure you remain committed to your goals. If your goal is specific, you know if you are on track or not. If your goal is measurable, you can see exactly where you are falling short. Later in the chapter, we'll also talk about how you can combine SMART goals with Stoic self-reflection to further build this sense of accountability and help you to remain motivated.

Moreover, SMART goals utilize modern psychology to help keep you focused. This aligns with Stoicism because it is an act of wisdom to use science to help you remain motivated. Furthermore, by making sure that your goals are attainable, you demonstrate wisdom in understanding yourself and living in accordance with your nature.

In addition to thinking about SMART goals, it is also important to align your goals with Stoic principles directly. This means choosing goals that are virtuous. For example, goals to bring ruin to another individual are entirely inappropriate for a modern Stoic. Remember that the act of setting a goal is another opportunity to act virtuously and to rise to the occasion that presents itself.

It goes without saying that you should avoid goals that are unvirtuous. A more subtle consideration is the idea that you should be careful about the limits of your control. Remember that a tenet of Stoicism is the importance of recognizing what lies in your control and what does not. This can be very important when setting goals. There is no wisdom in setting goals that are entirely reliant on external factors that fall out of your scope of influence. Stoicism instead advocates setting goals that are directed more inwardly, goals that work on your actions and reactions to external events.

Let's consider this idea in practice. Suppose you want to advance in your career. Although Stoicism would warn against the frantic pursuit of wealth above all else, it is not inappropriate to have career advancement as a goal. Career advancement can help you support your family and help your community, and it involves taking on greater responsibilities that may make you into a better man. So far, then, so good.

However, when thinking about career advancement and devising goals, it is important to make a goal that focuses on what lies within your control. Suppose you set the following goal, following SMART principles:

My goal is to be promoted to management in the company within 6 months.

This is specific, presumably attainable, relevant to your life, and time-bound. Some work might need to be done to make sure the goal is measurable, but that will depend on the particulars of your line of work.

However, this goal does not align with Stoic principles because whether or not you are promoted relies too much on factors that are beyond your control. For example, there will have to be a vacancy. No matter how well you perform at your job, if there isn't an opportunity for promotion, you are not going to be promoted. Alternatively, it depends on there not

82

being a better candidate available, or perhaps there not being one who is not only as qualified as you but who is also a family friend of your boss. There are hundreds of possible reasons why you might or might not get promoted within 6 months, most of which are completely beyond your control. Consequently, the goal is not wise according to Stoic principles.

That doesn't mean that you should give up on your ambition of career advancement. Instead, what it means is that your goals should be more focused on your conduct than on a particular achievement. For example, let's suppose that you are competent at your work, but you are a bit shy and struggle with meetings or group presentations. Despite being great at your job, it is hard for your bosses to notice you because of this shyness. This is then holding back your career advancement, so you might set the following goal:

My goal is to work on my interpersonal skills by volunteering to lead a meeting in my department at least once a month. I commit to doing this for at least 6 months.

This goal focuses on your own conduct and on improving yourself. You can combine it with other inward-focused goals that improve your job performance. Hopefully, it will lead to career advancement because your bosses will take notice of the hard work you are doing. However, even if it doesn't lead to career advancement—for all those external reasons that you cannot control—you still will have improved your interpersonal skills. You will have acted with courage to push yourself out of your comfort zone. You will have acted virtuously and worked on bettering yourself, and this will help you feel greater self-respect and fulfillment.

The trick, then, is to focus on goals that are under your influence. Look inward rather than outward and identify where you can improve and better yourself. Chances are good positive things will happen to you but ultimately it doesn't matter: You will have made yourself into a better man regardless.

Overcoming Obstacles

Of course, even if your goal could not be more SMART or more aligned with Stoic principles, you are sometimes going to fall short. If you are trying to get into shape, you'll miss a couple of days of exercise every now and again. If you are trying to work on your interpersonal confidence, sometimes you'll get tongue-tied or avoid a situation you should have grappled by the horns.

The first thing to say is that this is okay. Remember Tenet 9: We are aiming at progress, not perfection. It is okay to accept that you are not perfect. To beat yourself up excessively is not temperate, and it is not wise. In fact, it is likely to demotivate you further because you will start to associate your goals with negative, self-critical thoughts.

On the other hand, this doesn't mean that you shouldn't try to learn from your mistakes. You can extend forgiveness and kindness to yourself without accepting those shortcomings as permanent. Hold yourself accountable, show discipline, and work on your self-improvement.

This is where self-reflection comes in. Remember the self-reflection exercises from Chapter 4. If you are having difficulty with letting go of self-critical thoughts, consider using the view-from-above self-reflection or other mindfulness techniques to help ground you and give you a sense of perspective. Falling short of your goals isn't the end of the world, and every misstep is an opportunity for future improvement.

Then, think about what happened. You might use the self-reflection technique that considers the cognitive cycle and work to identify the behaviors, thoughts, feelings, and physical sensations that surrounded the slipup. This might help you identify what went wrong, allowing you to put strategies in place to avoid such mistakes in the future.

For example, let's suppose your goal is to do more exercise, but you've missed the workout you were meant to do today. It is too late to do it now, so first it is important to recognize that the misstep is now beyond your control. All you can dictate is how you react, so let go of guilt and self-recrimination and refocus your mind on constructive steps you can take to avoid this happening again.

Next, think about what happened. Take the perspective of an objective observer and try to identify what went wrong, considering your behaviors, what you were thinking, and how you were feeling at the time. Use a journal so you can write down your reflections. This will be useful if the problem recurs as you can start to review your reflections and find patterns. When analyzing the situation, consider simple steps you can take to prevent the same thing from happening again. You might not be able to identify anything in the first instance of the setback, but by writing down your reflections, you might be able to identify those patterns in the future.

Continuing the example, if you work out in the evenings, you might find that you tend not to exercise on those days when you've had a bad day at work. You might further reflect that you tend to feel physically tired on those occasions. This suggests that you should have a look at your sleep hygiene. This will help you to regulate your emotions, have a happier day at work, and be more motivated for evening exercise.

Continue to use self-reflection. Imagine that you are a scientist recording results. Getting enough sleep will probably help your situation, but there might be more you can do. Experiment with different solutions and strategies, combine them and see what works for you. Throughout, self-reflect and build up a greater understanding of your own nature so that you can apply that same wisdom for further advantages. Take this example: Failing to exercise one day has set you on a path to self-improvement.

At this point, I want to give special mention to one strategy that is often helpful for overcoming obstacles: asking for help. As men, we are sometimes discouraged from doing this because it is perceived as admitting weakness to our peers. Though you don't want to be entirely reliant on others, the truth is that asking for help every now and again demonstrates courage, justice, and wisdom.

It shows courage because we are opening up to another person, admitting to ourselves that we need assistance, and demonstrating that we are secure enough in ourselves to ask for help. It shows justice because it is fairer to ourselves to get assistance than to suffer in silence. Finally, it shows wisdom because it helps us acquire the skills and know-how to approach similar problems in the future.

Getting assistance doesn't mean that someone else fixes your problem for you: You can learn from the help they give and improve your own understanding of the problem and its solution. Asking for help also involves putting your ego to one side so you can approach the current problem in a constructive manner.

If you are not convinced, then consider the words of Marcus Aurelius (2006/161-180 A.D.): "Don't be ashamed to need help. Like a soldier storming a wall, you have a mission to accomplish. And if you've been wounded and you need a comrade to pull you up? So what?"

Of course, sometimes the solution to overcoming an obstacle is simply perseverance. Life is not always easy. The modern Stoic man recognizes when he needs to grit his teeth, maintain discipline, and get at it. Remember that every obstacle is an opportunity to take inspiration from the ancient Stoics, show your manliness and determination, and take the next step you need to take on your journey.

Achieving Personal and Professional Growth

By looking inward and focusing on your personal betterment, you will start to see improvements in your well-being and in your professional life. Rather than focusing on those elements of your life that you cannot control, you will take steps to excel in your career and personal conduct, becoming a better man in the process. Hopefully, others will take notice and career advancement will follow.

Sometimes, however, you may not see immediate benefits from your hard work. You might be passed over for promotion, or it might take longer than you hoped for you to lose that extra holiday weight. Worse yet, others might criticize you for your dedication, promising that a little indulgence is a one-off. They might have a go at you for not joining them in their own vices.

This is where another Stoic principle becomes important: euthymia. Translating to "a state of tranquility," euthymia is about staying the course and not being distracted by little setbacks or temptations. Seneca (2017/c.65 A.D.) wrote about the importance of "believing in yourself and trusting that you are on the right path, and not being in doubt by following the myriad footpaths of those wandering in every direction."

If you have chosen a goal that aligns well with Stoic principles, then you don't need to second-guess yourself. Maintain courage in your own convictions and hold to what you know is right and virtuous. Remember, too, that your true friends should inspire you to greater virtue, not deride you for trying to become a better man.

It is important to balance euthymia with self-reflection. Confidence in what you know is right is something worth protecting, but this is not the same thing as stubbornness. Sometimes you make mistakes; other times you might make a mistake in the goal you set. Reflect on the decisions you have made, not in relation to the complaints of indulgent or unsupportive friends but in relation to your own moral compass and wisdom.

In particular, remember that sometimes you will need to rest. Seneca (2017/c.65 A.D.) warned, "The mind must be given relaxation—it will rise improved and sharper after a good break." Bear this in mind, and don't push yourself to the brink of collapse. Think back to SMART goals and live according to your nature by making sure that your goals are attainable.

It can be a difficult balance to strike and be prepared to get that balance wrong every now and again. That's okay. Just make sure to self-reflect and to refine your behavior for constant self-improvement. Over time, you will start to recognize that your life is better. That you are better. You will continue to work on bettering yourself, but you will also be content with the knowledge that you are a man of integrity and self-respect. You will be healthier, more virtuous, and have an improved ability to regulate your emotions.

There will not be any particular point in time when all your problems are fixed and eudaemonia takes root, but over time, you will notice a gradual improvement and sense of fulfillment. When you notice it, allow yourself to pat yourself on the back—then get back to your journey.

A Template for Goal Setting

You can use this format as a template when setting goals that are in accordance with Stoic principles. Consider it a kind of checklist or self-reflection for making sure your goal is appropriate for your nature.

What is my goal?

- My goal is...

How is my goal virtuous?

- My goal demonstrates wisdom because...

- My goal demonstrates courage because...

- My goal demonstrates justice because...

- My goal demonstrates temperance because...

How is my goal SMART?

- My goal is specific because...

- My goal is measurable because...

- My goal is attainable because...

- My goal is relevant to me because...

- My goal is time-bound because...

Do I have control over whether I complete my goal?

- I have control over whether I complete my goal because...

- I recognize that some elements related to my goal are beyond my control and that it is unwise to focus on them. These elements are...

Chapter 8:
Health and Wellness

The ancient Stoics never thought that health and wellness were ends in themselves. Like with wealth, they believed that health could not be the true good because sometimes protecting your health is a bad action. The man who stands by and does nothing while a child drowns shows cowardice, even though he has protected his own health in the meantime.

The Stoics also practiced what they preached. When Seneca was wrongly implicated in a plot against Roman Emperor Nero, he obeyed his emperor's commands to kill himself, reasoning that justice and the functioning of the state were more important than his life.

However, throughout this book, we have talked about living according to your human nature. Primarily, this means living as a rational being and recognizing that you can control how you act and react to life's challenges. However, it also means having the wisdom to recognize what is good for you as a human being. This involves considering your health and wellness.

Your mental health and physical health are interrelated, and maintaining a healthy state makes it easier to act virtuously. Health may not be the true good, but it is *a* good, and it is part of a flourishing life. As per Tenet 4, it helps give you the tools to thrive. Relative improvement in health is also accessible to anyone.

In this chapter, we'll look at health and wellness and how the Stoics might approach the issue. We'll talk about the mind–body connection in a bit more detail, as well as consider some healthy habits and routines that you might implement.

A Stoic Approach to Physical and Mental Well-Being

It should come as no surprise that Stoicism advocates a virtue-based approach to physical and mental well-being. Like with career advancement, the Stoics warned against pursuing health to the neglect of everything else. However, there is nothing wrong with working on your health as long as your actions remain virtuous. Furthermore, working on your physical and mental well-being can be a great opportunity to practice virtuous actions.

In particular, working on your health may well involve temperance. If you are trying to lose weight, then you will use temperance to resist temptations to eat unhealthily or to put off going for a run. If you are working on your sleep hygiene, you will need temperance and discipline to keep to your new bedtime, and to persevere even when you are tempted to stay up for one last round of a game or episode of a TV show.

Though temperance may have a prominent role in your journey, you will also have to demonstrate wisdom and courage. You will need wisdom to recognize your physical limits so that you do not push yourself too hard or too fast. A great way of ruining a new health regimen is to approach it gung ho, which will result in injuries that bring the whole thing to a screeching halt.

Furthermore, you will utilize wisdom to recognize those habits that are appropriate for your nature and those that are not. In other words, you will utilize wisdom to identify parts of your health that you can work on.

You will also demonstrate courage. Grit and force of will may be required when you are confronted with a rainy day and considering whether to go for that run. Courage isn't just about life and death situations. It is also about holding yourself to account, persevering in the face of adversity, and doing your best regardless of external events that cause you hardship or setbacks.

When considering ways of improving your physical and mental well-being, you should also utilize the Stoic techniques already outlined in this book. For example, you should use self-reflection to identify potential pitfalls to your new regimen and to consider new ways of motivating yourself. You should use negative visualizations to recognize the cost of not keeping to your regimen and to ruminate on the potential disasters that bad health could bring. These include diabetes, heart disease, and an increased risk of stroke.

When thinking about your mental well-being, you should make use of mindfulness techniques to keep you grounded in the present and to help you avoid unnecessary stress that could impact your emotional regulation. Furthermore, you should use the view-from-above reflection to put your hardships into perspective. This perspective can help you to grit your teeth and get on with your run, even when you are tempted to throw in the towel.

You might also approach working on your health as a kind of voluntary hardship. Fasting is associated with various health benefits, such as helping you to lose weight, avoid insulin spikes and crashes associated with the development of diabetes, and maintain a consistent level of energy throughout the day (Mosley, 2018). It is also an exercise in self-control and temperance, helping you to practice virtue and strengthen your inner resolve.

Similarly, a rigorous exercise regimen might be approached as a voluntary hardship. Though the best exercise regimens try to find forms of exercise that are at least partly fun, approaching exercise as a challenge to overcome and prove your inner strength can be a way of practicing virtue and building self-respect.

Throughout, remember to identify what lies within your control and what lies beyond it. You can control whether or not you keep to your workout schedule, but you cannot control genetic predispositions to certain illnesses or your overall body type.

When forming your goals, remember to look inward. Don't focus on outcomes that are influenced by external events beyond your influence, but instead focus on how you are going to act and what you will commit yourself to. This will keep you focused on those areas of life that you can control so that you avoid wasted effort.

The Mind-Body Connection

Seneca was plagued with ill health throughout his life. As such, he thought about his wellness quite a lot, applying Stoicism to his situation. One of the insights he came to was that there was a connection between his mental health and his physical health, writing that, "Comforting thoughts contribute to a person's cure; anything which raises his spirits benefits him physically as well" (Seneca, 2017/c.65 A.D.).

This insight is supported by modern medicine, which has found that there is a strong relationship between physical and mental health (Ohrnberger et al., 2017). Long-term physical health conditions can produce mental health complications such as anxiety and depression, while those same mental health conditions can have a negative impact on your physical health.

Some of this is indirect. For example, depression can impact your enthusiasm for physical exercise, which in turn contributes to poor physical health. There is also evidence of direct effects. For instance, depression may directly result in raised levels of cortisol (Dispatch Health, 2019), known colloquially as the stress hormone. Cortisol is part of the immune system, but if it is chronically elevated, this can lead to the immune system becoming resistant to its effects. Your immune response is thus compromised. This, in turn, makes you more susceptible to illness.

You might also remember the cognitive cycle from Chapter 4. Physical sensations can affect how we feel and think. Chronic pain can result in long-term irritability and anger-management issues. Tiredness can affect our emotional regulation, meaning that we are less in control of our feelings than a Stoic might like.

In turn, our mental health impacts our ability to act virtuously. We have already talked about emotional regulation: Depression, anxiety, and other mental health complications can impact our ability to keep our emotions in check, resulting in impulsive, unreasoned actions. Furthermore, motivational disorders such as depression can make it all the more difficult to practice temperance.

Stoicism holds that you always have a choice—even if you have depression, you remain a rational human being, and you can control how you react to life's events. But if we are being realistic, we should recognize that mental health complications can seriously impact your ability to act in a virtuous manner. It is hard to find the courage to face the day when your depression keeps you bedbound. It is hard to care about justice when you are constantly angry about everything.

If you are struggling with mental health difficulties, then there is no wisdom in suffering alone without help. Trying to handle mental health challenges without medical help can be dangerous. Men represented 78.7% of all suicides in the United States between 2000 and 2020 (The Associated Press, 2023), partly because men are less likely to get help. This is a tragedy. The wise course is to seek out professional help that utilizes modern medical techniques. Moreover, if things are really bad, remember Seneca's words (2017/c.65 A.D.): "Sometimes even to live is an act of courage."

The best course of all, however, is to prevent mental health challenges from escalating to a dangerous state in the first place. Because of the mind-body connection, this means taking steps to improve your physical health, practicing mindfulness exercises to keep your stress under control, and self-reflecting daily to identify any difficulties that rise to the level of a mental health condition.

Physical and mental health is a difficult topic for a Stoic because there is an element to which your well-being is beyond your control. If you have a genetic predisposition to depression, then this is something you cannot change. However, what you do have control over is how you react to that fact. Managing your symptoms with regular exercise, good sleep hygiene, and a healthy diet can contribute positively to your mental health. Being mindful of your own state of mind can help you act on problems before they escalate.

Give yourself permission to look after yourself. If you are in good physical and mental condition, you will be better placed to look after the other people in your life and to provide for them in a virtuous manner. Furthermore, you are a human being, too. It is wise and just to provide for yourself and to ensure you live according to your nature.

Healthy Habits and Routines

In Chapter 3, we established some healthy habits you might put into place to work on your physical and mental well-being. Here, we expand on these routines, looking at three key areas: diet, exercise, and sleep.

Diet

Your diet affects both your physical health and your mental health. Joseph Firth and his colleagues at the University of Manchester (2020) found that healthy eating patterns are associated with better mental health when compared with unhealthy eating patterns, possibly relating to "the effects of certain foods or dietary patterns on glycemia, immune activation, and the gut microbiome." Meanwhile, we are all familiar with the effects of diet on physical health. The regular consumption of high-calorie, sugary foods can contribute to weight gain, diabetes, heart disease, and strokes (Rippe & Angelopoulos, 2016).

The modern Stoic man might experiment with different diets. Intermittent fasting meshes well with the Stoic ideals of temperance and voluntary hardship; it can also be an effective way of losing excess weight (Welton et al., 2020). However, it is also important to look at your daily diet and think about ways of making it a little healthier. As a start, most American men can afford to cut down on their carbohydrates. Consider if you can reduce the amount of bread and potatoes (including chips and fries) you eat, as well as sugary snacks such as chocolate or candy. If you can replace them with fruits and greens, all the better.

The problem with sugary carbohydrates is that they are high in glucose. When you consume a lot of glucose, your body needs to break down that glucose into energy, which it does using insulin. As a result, when you eat excessive amounts of carbohydrates, your body is flooded with insulin. If this happens regularly, then your body will begin to develop a resistance to insulin, resulting in type 2 diabetes. Furthermore, because glucose is a great source of energy, a high-carb diet will lead to excess energy that will be stored as fat in the liver, resulting in obesity and associated health complications.

In addition to looking at your diet wholesale, here are some small changes you can make to improve your health:

- **Don't eat after your evening meal:** We tend to only eat high-carb snacks, such as chips and candy, in the evening. By avoiding evening snacking, you might find that you can drastically cut down on your carb intake without feeling hungry or discomforted.

- **Eat a high-protein breakfast:** Another problem with high-carb meals is that the spike in insulin (to break down the glucose) will later result in an insulin crash. This crash is associated with feelings of irritability, tiredness, and hunger, all of which can tempt you to further snacking. With this in mind, it is important to choose a morning meal that avoids this insulin crash and maintains your energy for longer. High-protein meals are great for this because they take longer to break down and convert to energy in the body. More stable insulin levels are then maintained without the familiar spike and crash. Eggs are a particularly good breakfast protein, so consider scrambled eggs instead of cereal in the morning.

- **Consider soup:** Because of its high water content, soup can fill your stomach and leave you satiated without contributing a lot of calories. Studies show that having soup when you want to snack is associated with significant weight loss (Rolls et al., 2012), making it a great alternative to chips or candy.

Exercise

Regular exercise can help you stay in shape, cut down your weight, and improve your mental health (Warburton et al., 2006). When it comes to physical health, exercise can improve your general fitness while using calories that would otherwise be stored as fat as fuel. Exercise also causes your brain to release endorphins and serotonin, which can boost your mood, not to mention the positive mental health impact of good fitness and positive self-esteem that you benefit from.

An important thing to consider when it comes to regular exercise is your lifestyle and preferences. You are more likely to keep to a new exercise regimen if you enjoy the activity you are doing and it fits well into your existing schedule. If you like sports, then seek out a local group and exercise that way. If you are a gym rat, then embrace your passion. Don't force yourself to do a kind of exercise that you absolutely hate, at least not regularly. Forcing yourself to go for a run every now and again might be an effective form of voluntary hardship, but it is going to be very difficult to stick to on a regular basis if you dread it every time you put on your running shoes.

Similarly, think about your schedule. If you tend to work late on Thursdays, then don't sign up for a sports team that practices at that time. It sounds obvious, but it is easy to get caught up in the enthusiasm of committing to a new regimen without thinking through the practicalities. By paying attention to the logistics, you'll give yourself a better chance at staying motivated and committed.

Below are some other useful tips to think about when considering regular exercise:

- **Make exercise social:** A great way of making regular exercise more enjoyable is to make it a group activity. Exercising as a group can be an opportunity for socializing, helping you to work on your social health at the same time as your physical and mental well-being. Moreover, working out with others keeps you accountable to each other. This means that you can motivate one another when you need it.

- **Consider HIIT:** High-intensity interval training, or HIIT, is an effective way of getting regular exercise if you are on a tight schedule. HIIT works by asking you to do high-intensity exercise in short bursts. As a result, it takes up less time than other forms of exercise without costing you the health benefits (Atakan et al., 2021). Though it can be intense—after all, "intensity" is in the name—you can get your daily exercise done in 15 minutes from the convenience of your home, making it perfect for busy people. Search for HIIT exercises on YouTube to get started.

Sleep

Sleep is very easy to overlook. In our modern age, we tend to make a virtue out of not getting much sleep. We say that we are working so hard that we've barely slept, or that we get up extra early to get more things done in a day. However, this is a false virtue and is not living in accordance with our nature as rational human beings.

A psychology study by Susan L. Worley (2018) found that not getting enough sleep is associated with "a wide range of disorders, such as hypertension, obesity and type 2 diabetes, cardiovascular disease, impaired immune functioning, and more." In addition to these physical health implications of not getting enough sleep, researchers have found that improving sleep quality is correlated with improved mental health (Scott et al., 2021).

In short, not getting enough sleep is not a virtue: It is unwise, leads to health complications, and ultimately makes you less efficient in those other tasks you were losing out on sleep for. If you get enough sleep, you'll be more functional and in control of your emotions. You'll be more efficient at your work and completing your family responsibilities, meaning that what you lose on time for sleeping, you'll more than gain in productivity.

As it is, many of us neglect our sleep health simply by not thinking about it. Whether we decide to keep watching TV when we should go to bed or allow ourselves to sleep in on the weekend, we tend not to realize that we are impacting our sleep hygiene and affecting the quality of the rest we get.

The number one thing to think about when it comes to sleep is habit and repetition. Set a bedtime and a time you'll get up each day, giving yourself at least 7 hours of slumber, and try to stick to it even over the weekend. It is okay to have a bit of flexibility—for example, if your buddies always meet up on a Friday night, it is okay to balance sleep health with your social well-being. However, try to resist having a lie-in just for the sake of it or going to bed late just because you lost track of time.

A common misconception is that you can somehow make up for sleep missed in the week by sleeping in at the weekend. This isn't how the body works, but keeping to a fixed sleep schedule does improve the quality of your sleep and makes it easier to fall asleep when you want to.

The following tips are also useful when thinking about improving the quality of your sleep:

- **Remove all screens from the bedroom:** We talked about this in Chapter 3. Screens contain blue light that signals to the brain that it is daytime, while the social media we browse tends to activate the mind when it should be winding down. Try imposing a blanket rule against screens in the bedroom and reserve your bed for sleeping and intimacy.

- **Avoid eating a few hours before bed:** Not only does eating after your evening meal tend to involve unhealthy snacks, but it also gives your body a boost of energy when it should be getting ready for rest. Avoid eating a few hours before your bedtime, and your body will be more ready for relaxing and consistent sleep. Furthermore, avoid caffeine for around 6 hours before bed, as it is a stimulant and takes around this long to leave your system.

- **Consider taking a bath 90 minutes before bed:** Studies suggest that taking a bath or relaxing shower an hour or two before going to bed can help you fall asleep more easily (Neilson, 2019). This is because getting out of the bath afterward lowers your core temperature, which is a signal to your brain that it is soon time to sleep (mimicking the temperature effects of nightfall).

Chapter 9:

Stoicism and Creativity

FROM STRUGGLE, INSPIRATION, FROM FAILURE, CREATION

We rarely think of ancient philosophy and creativity as connected. However, the ancient Stoics were concerned with the best way to live, and no account of human life is complete without considering our innate imaginativeness.

Humans are naturally creative. Our kind rose to dominance by repurposing objects we found in the wild into tools. We have constructed cities and brought novel solutions to problems that other species cannot even comprehend. We experiment with art and prose and film. We explore the nature of what it is to be human with novels and poems. Stoicism holds that we should live according to our nature as rational beings, and, if we're going to live according to our nature, we must also live as creative beings.

In this chapter, we look at more links between Stoicism and creativity and consider how to unlock your creative potential. We'll also discuss how to overcome creative blocks and how failure should be embraced as an opportunity for both virtue and learning.

Unlocking Creative Potential

With its focus on self-reflection, inner wisdom, and grateful thought, Stoicism meshes well with artistic pursuits that seek to explore the beauty that is around us. The best art tends to mean something to the creator, whether it be a song about a deeply personal experience or a painting that tries to capture the feeling of awe we feel when we look at nature.

With this in mind, use your reflection and gratitude exercises as opportunities to explore the beauty of the world and get your creative juices flowing. You might even want to incorporate some creative writing into your exercises, expounding more poetically on those elements of the world you are grateful for. Think about what gives your life meaning, what you feel deeply about, and how you might be able to express these feelings to others in a creative manner.

These exercises may feel strange at first. As men, we are told to deal with practical concerns rather than express our feelings through poetry or song. However, another important part of Stoicism is being true to your nature without worrying about the opinions of others. As Marcus Aurelius (2006/161-180 A.D.) wrote: "Does anything genuinely beautiful need supplementing? No more than justice does—or truth, or kindness, or humility. Are any of those improved by being praised? Or damaged by contempt? Is an emerald suddenly flawed if no one admires it?"

Think of your creative expression as a kind of virtue, and do not be concerned with seeking praise or internalizing criticism. If you wish to work on your creative skills, it is fine to consider ways of improving your art, but equally, you don't have to worry about that if you don't want to. Exploring your creative side is an end in itself. You don't have to be the next Michelangelo.

This all connects to the importance of being able to distinguish that which you can control and that which you cannot. If you choose to share your creative outputs with others, you can't control how your art will be received. You cannot control whether they will love it or hate it, and so you should stop trying to chase external validation. Instead, focus on what the creative enterprise means to you. Use your creativity to explore the beauty of the world, to understand yourself and the human condition a little better, and to pursue wisdom with courage and temperance.

In addition to letting go of what you cannot control, you should not be seeking out praise at all. Marcus Aurelius (2006/161-180 A.D.) asked, "What is to be prized? An audience clapping? No. No more than the clacking of their tongues. Which is all that public praise amounts to—a clacking of tongues." Your self-worth should not come from external validation. Whether you receive it is outside of your control and is an unstable foundation on which to build self-respect. Instead, your self-respect should come from within, from your sense of virtue and integrity that makes you the kind of man you are. Marcus Aurelius also had a quotation for that: "It never ceases to amaze me: we all love ourselves more than other people but care more about their opinion than our own."

If you need a little help in letting go of the need for external validation, consider using Stoic exercises to assist you in finding the right perspective. The view-from-above reflection will help you understand that the praise of a stranger is insignificant when compared to the majesty of the cosmos and the complexity of the world.

Finally, when thinking about unlocking your creative potential, try to be proactive. Don't put it off for another day. As Seneca (2017/c.65 A.D.) wrote, "We must seize what flees." Life is too short to waste your time on procrastinating and worrying about whether your ideas are creative enough or whether your skills are good enough. Unless you are trying to get into a creative career, it doesn't matter how skilled you are as a musician or how adept you are with a paintbrush. Just experiment, express yourself, and follow your creativity where it leads.

Overcoming Creative Blocks

All artists experience creative blocks. The most famous of these is the dreaded writer's block: When the author can do nothing but stare at the screen, wondering what to write next.

Different artists tend to have different tips and tricks for overcoming creative blocks, but these tend to have a common theme: Just keep going. All artists will edit and revise their work. The writer will write their first draft and then edit and rewrite it. The artist will sketch out shapes and experiment before filling them in with paint. The musician will find particular riffs or sequences of notes and then constantly rearrange and refine them. The point is that the first draft of something doesn't have to be any good, even if you are a creative professional.

Creativity is a state of mind, and, to some extent, you can fake it until you make it. Forcing yourself to put something down on the page can get the creative juices flowing, even if you end up ripping up your first efforts and starting again with a renewed sense of vigor. Just keep going, and push through that wall. If you are not feeling very creative, then your creative output might not be very good. But you will have made the framework on which your creativity can build.

Of course, Stoicism has something to say about this kind of grit and perseverance. The ancient Stoics advocated determination and discipline in all things, writing that it was virtuous to persevere in the face of external hardship. To some extent, we cannot control when we encounter a creative block. All we can control is how we respond to it. The right and virtuous reaction is to push through. Even an artistic block is an opportunity for virtue and self-improvement. Or, as Marcus Aurelius (2006/161-180 A.D.) put it, "The impediment to action advances action. What stands in the way becomes the way."

Similarly, if you are facing motivational issues when it comes to your creativity, it is worth reflecting on your proper nature according to Stoic principles. You are a man, you are a citizen of the world, and you have something to offer.

Admiral William H. McRaven gave a now-famous commencement speech to students from the University of Texas in 2014. In his speech, he struck a profoundly Stoic tone and offered some great advice for overcoming motivational difficulties (McRaven, n.d.):

If you make your bed every morning, you will have accomplished the first task of the day. It will give you a small sense of pride, and it will encourage you to do another task and another and another. By the end of the day, that one task completed will have turned into many tasks completed. Making your bed will also reinforce the fact that little things in life matter. If you can't do the little things right, you will never do the big things right.

And, if by chance you have a miserable day, you will come home to a bed that is made—that you made—and a made bed gives you encouragement that tomorrow will be better.

If you want to change the world, start off by making your bed. (para 17–19)

Embracing Failure as a Learning Opportunity

There is no creative success without failure. Indeed, there might be no success at all without failure. The most successful people in the world have all experienced missteps: Bill Gates's first company was a failure,

Michael Jordan was cut from his high school basketball team, and Ariana Huffington was turned down by 36 publishers. To some extent, what made these individuals successful is that they experienced that failure and learned from the experience.

Of course, Stoicism is less concerned with renown and success in the traditional sense. Fame is fleeting: Do you know the name of the most famous actor in 1850? Do you know the most famous musician from 80 years ago? Stoicism teaches that it is worth rising above this kind of praise and success and recognizing them as irrelevant. It teaches to avoid becoming obsessed with matters that are beyond our control. What Stoicism is concerned with is how you can continue your path to self-improvement, and this is a path that will have successes and failures like any other.

We've talked to some extent about failure in earlier chapters. When considering your self-reflections, part of the point is to recognize where you fell short and didn't act as you would like to have acted. Stoicism advocates self-reflection so these failures can be identified, and strategies can be put in place to avoid similar failures in the future. We cannot change the past, but we can control how we respond to our past mistakes. We can commit to self-improvement and resolve not to make the same mistakes again.

Like this, then, failure is a learning opportunity. Using Stoic exercises, it is important to recognize where something has gone wrong because these failures are often far more instructive than successes will be. When it comes to creative endeavors, these failures might range from the entirely practical to the ethical. You might have been too hasty with a paintbrush stroke, giving you an opportunity to learn the value of taking your time and showing temperance and restraint. Alternatively, you might come to disagree with the sentiment of a poem you've written, finding it too complaining and unvirtuous.

The important thing is not to bring a sense of shame or recrimination to this process. Remember that you cannot change the past, so it is unwise to regret what has already happened. What you can control is your response, so your focus should not be on self-blame but on self-improvement. Embracing your creativity is all about personal growth and self-exploration, so come to the endeavor with humility and grace.

If you are new to a creative pursuit, you can expect to fail often. That's just another way of saying that you'll do a lot of learning. You'll learn that certain phrases are cliched or trite, that hastiness can be counterproductive, or that certain artistic impulses are shallow and unvirtuous.

Yet, just as failure is an opportunity for learning, it is also an opportunity for virtue. Have the wisdom to learn from your mistakes, the courage to persevere when those mistakes are many, the justice to absolve yourself for the errors of a novice, and the temperance to take all these lessons in good grace. Even if you never rise to the level of a world-renowned painter, you will have become a better man in the process.

Exercises for Boosting Creativity

In this section, we outline a few useful exercises that might be considered for getting those creative juices flowing:

- **Consider your purpose:** In your next self-reflection, think about what you care deeply about and write down what matters to you. This might range from the specific, such as your family, to something more ephemeral, like the beauty of nature or the profundity of virtue. Next time you are engaged in a creative activity, try to express those feelings on the page.

- **Use a prompt:** A quick search on the Internet will provide many writing prompts for getting started. Use these to help you get started, whether that be in prose, music, or visual art.

- **Think about existing self-reflections:** Your gratitude exercises or the view-from-above self-reflection can help you boost your creative impulses. Look back over past exercises and consider whether any of your reflections speak to you in a creative way—either by giving you a sense of awe about the majesty of the cosmos or providing inspiration to make art about a particular part of the human condition.

Part 4:

Everyday Challenges and Community

Each of us dwell, in effect, in two communities—the local community of our birth, and the community of human argument and aspiration that is truly great and truly common, in which we look neither to this corner nor to that, but measure the boundaries of our nation by the sun. –Lucius Seneca

In the final part of the book, we will consider the three remaining tenets of Stoicism, which are of particular importance for living within a community and dealing with everyday challenges:

- Tenet 6: Rationality in the world and in ourselves: Accept responsibility

- Tenet 7: No man is an island. We are part of the world

- Tenet 8: We can only grow when we are part of something greater

To live according to our nature is to live as a cosmopolitan—a citizen of the world. Stoicism holds that we are part of a whole, not an autonomous entity and that we have a duty to nature and the world around us.

Wisdom holds that what affects our community will affect us, so we must serve our community in order to serve ourselves. To put it another way, in the words of Marcus Aurelius (2006/161-180 A.D.): "That which is not good for the beehive cannot be good for the bees."

Justice demands that we do not serve ourselves alone but seek ways of bringing virtue to the community about us, taking no more than a fair share of resources for ourselves.

Meanwhile, courage means we must stand beside individuals who need our help: Individuals who are underprivileged, or in a position of vulnerability. Sometimes, standing up for the little guy in society will expose you to mockery. You cannot control that. All you can control is how you act and behave, and by choosing virtuous action, you will flourish.

Finally, an adherence to temperance reminds us that there is no true good to be found in objects and things. It is only through virtuous action and taking our rightful part in the world that we can achieve the contentment of eudaemonia.

As noted in Chapter 1, men are sometimes raised to think that extreme self-sufficiency is a virtue. Of course, self-sufficiency is positive, but when it is taken to an extreme, it can be both intemperate and unwise. A man who tries to walk off a broken leg is not acting sensibly.

Being a cosmopolitan isn't just about asking for help when you need it. It is also about partaking in social projects and helping to build great things through co-operation and mutual effort. The greatest cities were built by thousands of hands. Behind every great act of creation was a legion of teachers, artisans, and patrons who helped a genius to create their magnum opus.

Closer to home, any important work project or substantial home improvement effort requires co-operation. By adopting your role in these projects, you become part of something greater and find opportunity for virtue. You learn, show your strength, and grow.

In Part 4, we'll consider two key topics: How the modern Stoic man handles contemporary challenges with respect to new technologies and how he should take an active role in his community.

Chapter 10:
Contemporary Challenges and Stoic Solutions

Through technology, we have achieved amazing things. In the space of just 100 years, humanity went from not being able to fly to reaching the moon. The Internet has profoundly changed the nature of communication, allowing humans to speak with other humans on the other side of the world and share ideas and perspectives. Vehicles allow us to traverse distances that would have been unthinkable to our ancestors only a few generations ago.

And yet, technology has proved a double-edged sword. The Space Race was a militaristic contest between two superpowers that constantly threatened to destroy the world. The vehicles we have built have poisoned our atmosphere and caused irreversible climate change. The Internet has led to an explosion of misinformation and online bullying.

In this chapter, we look at the challenges posed by modern technology and discover that the lessons of ancient Stoicism still apply. The Internet—especially social media—is effectively designed to provoke us to unvirtuous action. However, by remaining true to our sense of virtue, we can overcome these challenges and be the better men.

Navigating the Digital Age: Mindfulness in a Connected World

The Internet is largely funded by advertising. From social media to news organizations, the success of these websites depends on you clicking on pages and staying on them. As such, you are more likely to see the adverts or tolerate an advert that cannot be skipped or clicked away. These websites, then, are in the game of stealing your attention and are powered by AI learning models that work to manipulate our base natures to that purpose.

It isn't that AI is fundamentally evil. It's just that models have been programmed to maximize engagement, and it turns out that appealing to our worst nature is the most effective way to do that. Let's take one relatively simple example. Human beings have a negative bias, so we attend more to negative stimuli than positive stimuli (Vaish et al., 2008). This is an evolutionary bias because the early human beings who attended to potential threats were more likely to survive to procreate than those early human beings who were hopelessly optimistic. The early humans who thought a rustling bush was a sabretooth or rattlesnake may have been wrong 99% of the time, but they were certainly prepared for that crucial 1% occurrence.

How does this relate to the Internet and modern technology? Well, though sabretooth tigers may have gone away, our negative bias hasn't. And it still influences how we act and think. We are more likely to click on news headlines that contain negative words (Robertson et al., 2023). This means that we are more inclined to engage with negativity on the Internet than positivity, so algorithms fill our recommendations with pessimistic headlines and article titles. The goal of the algorithm is just to have us click, but it works by taking advantage of instinctive behaviors. In other words, it works by bypassing our capacity for reason, undermining the virtues of wisdom and temperance.

Unfortunately, this is not the limit of the problem. AI algorithms have also discovered that slowly escalating the extremity of the content it recommends is an effective way of maintaining engagement (Camargo, 2020). From a starting point of reasonable skepticism about the dangers of the pharmaceutical industry, a left-of-center user might be radicalized into full-blown, anti-science vaccine denial. This has contributed to the polarization of our society, which, of course, leads to ever greater engagement online. If you've ever been pulled into an Internet argument, you will understand how addictive such disagreements can be.

These, then, are some of the problems. The good news is that they have solutions. By considering the tenets of Stoicism, we can overcome these challenges and maintain our sense of virtue. The fundamental thing we need to internalize is that we must live according to our nature. We are rational beings, and though the Internet attempts to bypass our reason, we ultimately have the choice in how we react and feel about negative headlines and clickbait articles. As Tenet 6 advocates, we must take responsibility for our own actions and consider what is virtuous when confronted with such tactics.

The key is mindfulness. The game is all about attention: The Internet tries to usurp our attention, but we should not cede that power to algorithms in the service of advertisers. Mindfulness exercises are a great way of practicing how to control and redirect our thoughts. The 4-7-8 breathing technique, body scan, and other exercises work by bringing our awareness to our breathing or other sensations in our bodies.

The more you practice them, the better you will be at focusing your attention and redirecting it when you are distracted by an intrusive thought. This, in turn, will empower you against the tactics of algorithms because you will not be so easily drawn in by clickbait, conspiracy theories, and negativity. You will maintain control and responsibility for your actions and make use of the rational space between stimulus and action.

In addition to these mindfulness techniques, you can also make use of self-reflection exercises to better understand your triggers and temptations and put in place strategies for your self-improvement. Recognizing the kinds of articles that are particularly distracting or tempting can be an effective way of removing their power. Once you realize that you are being manipulated, that manipulation is less likely to work against you.

You can also use recontextualization to help process what is going on. Next time you are confronted with a nonsense story about two famous people getting into some feud, recontextualize it to try to look at the matter more objectively. An AI-learning algorithm has determined that misrepresenting the words of two human beings can give the impression of a conflict; this in turn appeals to your primitive evolutionary instincts, so you click on the article and generate more revenue for the website from advertisers. By reframing and understanding what is going on, you can overcome temptations and rediscover the wisdom of not clicking.

Managing Technology and Social Media

We've talked about the pitfalls of the Internet and modern technology and touched on some potential Stoic solutions. In this section, we'll have a bit more of a think about the four cardinal virtues and how they can be applied to social media.

By practicing mindfulness, you can reclaim your ability to act according to your nature and maintain control over how you react and behave on social media. From there, you can make the choice to act in a way that is virtuous.

When it comes to the Internet, wisdom is all about not ceding control to algorithm-created impulses and thinking before you click. It may seem harmless to click on a silly article that's clearly clickbait, but, if you are wise, you will recognize that this is the precipice of a slippery slope. Giving in to temptation now will make you more susceptible to temptation later. Wisdom suggests that you should not click and instead devote your time to activities that are more enriching and fulfilling. You are responsible for how you spend your time, and you can choose not to waste it on pointless listicles or misinformation.

If you are committed to wisdom, you will also learn to be more discerning about information provided online. We all know that misinformation is rife on social media. Take the time to educate yourself on how to evaluate information so you can avoid being suckered in by false narratives.

Always consider the source of the information and whether it tallies with the information offered by alternative sources that you trust. Importantly, always be distrustful of content that seems designed to confirm your political opinions. Reality doesn't have a political viewpoint, so any news article that is clearly right wing or left wing is probably biased. Think about what the motivations of the writer might be and whether their intention is to inform or to persuade.

Next, let's talk about temperance. Perhaps more than anything else, modern technology is designed to bypass our sense of temperance. Algorithms are designed to encourage you to act impulsively: to engage with content regardless of the wisdom or utility of doing so. Temperance is about resisting those impulses and instead choosing what is good for your fundamental nature. It is about avoiding Internet addiction, focusing your attention on one thing rather than allowing yourself to be distracted, and remaining disciplined in the face of a chaotic world.

If you think you may be somewhat addicted to social media, spending hours on it every day, recognize that this is an opportunity to practice temperance. Cut down on your hours and stop using your phone when you're in bed. If you are used to endlessly browsing Facebook or TikTok, this adjustment will require discipline, but you will become a better man for it.

In addition, practice temperance when it comes to online debates. One of the problems with these arguments is that there is no sense of accountability. The Internet doesn't feel quite real, and we don't fully internalize that we are talking to real people with real feelings and emotions. It doesn't help that half the contributors to the conversation are bots!

However, even if you are talking to a procedurally generated bot, you should conduct yourself as you would if you were speaking to another human being in person. By practicing temperance, you can keep your cool, remain civil, and avoid hyperbole or exaggeration. Try not to care about the number of likes your comment gets because such approval is ephemeral and does not connect to any stable sense of self-respect or integrity. Refocus on your own conduct and what you can control.

This brings us to courage. When it comes to the Internet, courage is all about honesty and integrity. Social media and news websites have contributed to a tribal mindset where we are all supposed to parrot the views of a political tribe that we are told we belong to. We see things increasingly in black and white when in fact the world and politics are nuanced and contain shades of gray.

Don't let an algorithm put you into a political box. Demonstrate your courage and think for yourself. Most people have a variety of political views, some of which are left wing and some of which are right wing. Even if you tend to vote one way rather than the other, that doesn't mean you have to give up those opinions that tally more with the other side's position. Don't seek the comfort of the group. Remain true to your own beliefs. This may cost you likes and reposts, but you will have maintained your integrity.

Finally, let's think about justice. The Internet has a tendency to encourage mob justice because of the way social media polarizes and anonymizes. We are encouraged to join our tribe and to forget the humanity of those in other groups. And, unfortunately, it can feel good to defend the group and pillory people who break faith with the social contract.

This book is not here to give an opinion on cancel culture or to espouse a particular political position. Stoicism asks you to make these judgments for yourself: to listen to other points of view and amend your opinion accordingly but to ultimately reach your own decisions based on your values.

However, without commenting on the rights and wrongs of public condemnation, we can still consider some questions that you should be asking yourself before participating. Are you acting justly when you add your voice to the criticisms? Are you speaking up because of your innate sense of right and wrong, or just because it feels good to be part of the crowd? And, most importantly of all, is the public condemnation in question fair, or is it bullying?

Finding Balance and Presence

We have talked about the dangers of the Internet and how they might be overcome by acting mindfully and virtuously. However, Stoicism does not ask you to oppose all forms of technology. Technology has empowered us to do incredible things, and it is important to find balance in our judgments.

It is a form of intemperance to allow our distrust of social media to infect our opinion of all technology. Everything must be judged separately and objectively. Furthermore, it is important to recognize what lies within our control and what falls beyond it. Railing against modern technology is one thing, but we are unable to halt the march of progress. Rather than wasting our time complaining, we must instead think about what we can control—that is, how we will behave and remain virtuous in the modern world.

For example, Stoicism doesn't ask that you abandon the Internet entirely. When used properly, the Internet can be a great way of learning new information and discovering new perspectives. It can be a tool for practicing wisdom and empathy for your fellow human beings. If you bring wisdom and temperance to your online dealings, you can unlock the true potential of this incredible technology. That means rising above the pointless chatter, engaging politely with other rational people, and utilizing the Internet as a source of endless information and data.

You have control. The algorithm may play into your base nature, but it is also receptive to your choices. If you ignore the clickbait and pointless negativity, then the algorithm will learn that you are not tempted by such things. If you instead click on articles about philosophy or engage in conversations about important ideas, you will start to see more of them appearing in your recommendations.

Don't trust the algorithm blindly, of course—it is important to remain discerning—but work with it to cultivate a virtuous space on the Internet for you to inhabit. Take responsibility and take control.

Finally, remember not to inhabit the Internet to the exclusion of all else. Psychologists have established that face-to-face social interaction is more important for psychological well-being than online social interaction (Hall et al., 2021). Maintain your presence in the physical world, connect with people you meet in your daily life, and don't seek to replace your social life with online interaction. That way, you will continue to flourish and achieve your own sense of eudaemonia.

Chapter 11:
Stoicism and the Greater Good

Stoicism is sometimes considered an inward-facing philosophy. It asks the modern Stoic man to focus on what he can control, to maintain discipline against the external pressures of the world, and to control how he reacts and feels to those external events that act upon him.

We can see how this would lead someone to the impression that Stoicism is silent on those external injustices that confront society. After all, as ordinary citizens, we cannot control the influence of money in politics. We cannot singlehandedly undo the gerrymandering of political districts or, in one stroke, fix the legacy of racial inequalities that lie in the history of our nation. These are all things beyond our control, so we might think that Stoicism would advocate a kind of apathy. We might think that Stoicism holds that we should be unaffected by these systematic inequalities because we are in no position to do anything about them.

However, this is too pessimistic a conclusion. The Stoic man is not passive but active, and though he may not be able to fix everything himself, that doesn't let him off the hook for small acts of justice that benefit his community. In this chapter, we consider this idea in more detail and explore how the modern Stoic man should engage with society.

Stoicism and the Greater Good

The ancient Stoics had a concept of *oikeiôsis*, the method by which the concerns of the individual are expanded until they share in the concerns of the individual's wider community. It is almost a psychological theory of social development rather than a philosophical precept, holding that human beings are born selfish as infants but that we start to expand our concerns beyond our immediate needs.

We realize that those in our immediate circle—such as our parents—have their own needs, and we begin to empathize with others. As we mature and explore our faculties of reason, we begin to understand that all human beings have individual concerns, and we begin to empathize with strangers that we don't know.

This is oikeiôsis, the ever-greater expansion of a circle of concern. It is underpinned by the simple observation that all human beings are alike in rationality and dignity. Once we combine this notion with the idea of a cosmopolitan, or citizen of the world, we start to get a sense of what Stoicism would say about the greater good.

By Tenet 7, no man is an island: We are part of the world. To live according to your nature is to live as a member of a species that is inherently connected by its common faculties of reason and virtue. All human beings—regardless of sex, gender, sexual preference, race, creed, or socioeconomic situation—are capable of acting in accordance with virtue, and as such, have innate worth that should be respected.

This is the lynchpin of justice, one of the cardinal virtues of Stoicism. It is the idea that we belong to one community of the species and that to do right by others is to do right by ourselves. By acting justly, we practice virtue and so flourish.

Furthermore, the Stoics believed in Tenet 8: You can only grow when you are part of something greater. In the eyes of Stoicism, working for the greater good cannot be separated from your personal flourishing. It is your proper nature to participate in your community, to be a social animal that co-operates with their fellow human beings. Hence, there is no conflict between Stoicism and looking outward to your community. As Marcus Aurelius (2006/161-180 A.D.) put it:

A branch cut from its neighboring branch is necessarily cut away from the whole tree. In the same way, a human being severed from just one other human has dropped from the whole community. Now the branch is cut off by someone else, but a man separates himself from his neighbor by his own hatred or rejection, not realizing that he has thereby severed himself from the wider society of fellow citizens. (11.8)

Civic Engagement

Yet there still seems to be some kind of conflict between wisdom and justice when it comes to civic engagement. After all, how can the modern Stoic man take steps to combat injustice in society when he knows that systematic injustice is ultimately an external event that lies beyond his control?

The squaring of this circle is to recognize that social progress is achieved step by step, not in huge leaps. Wisdom holds that you cannot control all social inequality, but this doesn't let you off the hook when it comes to behavior that contributes to this social inequality, nor does it release you from the responsibility of engaging and doing your part. As long as you recognize that your efforts are only one small part of a greater project, per Tenet 8, you can advocate for justice without sacrificing wisdom.

What you should resist, however, are impotent sweeping gestures or pointless complaining. Attempting such gestures is unwise and hubristic because it assumes that you have more control over social inequality than you actually possess. Meanwhile, complaining about social inequality without doing anything about it is empty rhetoric. Stoicism asks you to take responsibility, through Tenet 6, and step up. Contribute to the conversation and help out in local community projects, but don't just snipe from the sidelines.

At the very least, you should participate in the democratic process. You cannot control that at least a third of the population doesn't vote (Pew Research Center, 2023), but you can control whether *you* vote and whether you are part of the problem or part of the solution. Partake in civic engagement and exercise your rights to help strengthen the democracy you belong to.

Furthermore, consider the concept of oikeiôsis, and apply it to your own life in a deliberate fashion. Try to expand your circle of concern one step at a time. You may not be able to impact national politics in a meaningful way, but you might be surprised by the amount of control you have to impact your local community in a positive manner.

For example, you might consider a local problem of your borough or maybe just your street and take it upon yourself to fix the problem. Organize community crowdfunding, local charitable events, or simply speak to your neighbors about mutual steps you can take to make your community better. Stoicism asks you to consider what lies within your control and not what lies beyond your control, but this tenet is not wholly negative. When it comes to civic engagement, more lies in your power than you realize.

Ethical Considerations

The ethical considerations of the modern world may share some commonalities with the ancient world, but these commonalities are not all-encompassing. Our ethical sensibilities have changed since the time of the ancient Stoics, and that's okay—good, even. In modern America, slavery is considered a moral evil, democracy is viewed as sacrosanct, and we oppose prejudice in all its forms.

Of course, things are not always so simple. To take just one example, there is often lively social discussion about what prejudice is and how it is best combated. This conversation continues and ranges from the productive to the ugly. However, the point remains that our ethical sensibilities have evolved.

We can look to the philosophy of Stoicism and respect the ancient Stoics without pretending that they were saints. Marcus Aurelius was a Roman Emperor: No one voted for him, and those who resisted the might of his empire were put to death in bloody wars. Seneca may have advocated for treating slaves with more compassion, but he was still himself a slaveholder. The ancient Stoics had wisdom that is still relevant today, but that doesn't mean that they were perfect.

Remember that the basic philosophy of Stoicism is that you must take responsibility for your actions. To live in accordance with your nature is to embrace your innate rationality and to live relative to your own values and understanding of the virtues. Nowadays, we do not consider dictatorship or slavery to be just. We live to our own principles of what we think goodness is, and all Stoicism asks us to do is to defend those principles with integrity.

The modern world brings its own ethical considerations. A hot-button issue is the idea of cancel culture and the appropriateness of public backlash against perceived instances of injustice. There are many nuances to consider. On one hand, there are abuses and systematic inequalities that have been brought to light through so-called cancel culture, resulting in real-world positive change. On the other hand, public backlash has a tendency to get out of control, and there are instances of it being unleashed on individuals who did not deserve the severity of the condemnation.

This book will not tell you what to think about these matters. Stoicism asks you to think about these issues for yourself and to reach your own conclusions based on your understanding of wisdom, courage, justice, and temperance. However, one thing this book will do is to warn you against knee-jerk reactions. Remember that you are a rational being and there is space between an external event and how you feel about it, space in which you can think about the issue and reach your own, reasoned conclusion.

Moreover, try not to throw the baby out with the bathwater. The truth is that difficult ethical problems tend to be nuanced. After all, if they were not nuanced, they would not be difficult. Have the courage to recognize that there is plenty about an issue that you might not yet understand and have the wisdom to avoid sweeping judgments, no matter what you might see on social media or on your nightly news.

Eric O. Scott from Modern Stoicism (2016) advocates the principle of "philosophical charity." Philosophical charity is underpinned by the idea that the best criticism of a position is one that understands the position as charitably as possible. It is underpinned by the idea that good philosophical critique is about a mutual search for the truth rather than about keeping score in an argument.

Let's consider this in an example. Suppose that someone online makes a series of claims about systematic inequality against Black people in the workplace. You happen to know that some of their claims are factually false: Perhaps they are using statistics that have been discredited. However, the thrust of their overall argument remains supported by other, more credible statistics. How should you engage with their position?

Philosophical charity holds that you should ignore those little mistakes and errors that do not really matter to the overall argument. You should engage with the meat of the issue, considering the evidence and reasoning fairly. In this example, then, you shouldn't bring up the false statistic other than to gently inform the user that, while there are other statistics supporting their position, this particular piece of evidence is discredited. Rather than quibbling about minor points, you should engage with their overall argument, representing it as charitably as possible.

It sounds straightforward enough, but this kind of philosophical charity is rare, especially on the Internet. Consider how many threads you have read where one poster criticizes another poster for their spelling or grammar rather than engaging with what they are actually saying. These interactions aren't about charity or mutual discussion: They are about point-scoring, and they are unvirtuous.

Community Involvement

We've talked about oikeiôsis and how you might expand your circle of concern from your family and friends to your local community. In this section, we talk a bit more about this idea and also the concept of protesting.

Your local community will have its issues, which a little bit of reflection will undoubtedly expose. Maybe there is an issue with litter or graffiti: A relatively minor problem, but one that might still be affecting you and your neighbors and causing ecological damage to the world. Maybe your community suffers from a more serious problem, such as homelessness, crime, or overt acts of racism.

Before you leap into dealing with these issues, apply Stoic wisdom to these problems. Start by reflecting on them and identifying the challenges at their source. Instead of taking to the Internet to gripe, think about what the solutions to these problems might be and whether those solutions lie within your control.

Let's take a relatively minor example: littering. Littering can be unsightly, can attract pests such as rats, and can prevent the proper recycling of resources. When you see littering, your first instinct might be to get angry about the inconsiderateness of your neighbors. Instead, temper that emotion and take the time to think about what could help. Maybe there aren't enough trashcans, or there is a particular part of the street outside the deli where there is no trashcan and the litter piles up.

You might not be able to control the tendency people have to be inconsiderate, but getting a trashcan put outside the establishment may well lie within your control. You can speak to your local representative, organize a petition, or simply donate a small trashcan for the deli owners to put outside their front door. By thinking the matter through and acting in a deliberate, productive way, you can involve yourself in your community and be a force for positive change, no matter how small.

Of course, not all community problems are so minor or localized. It is relatively easy to get a new trashcan, but it's much harder to deal with rampant homelessness caused by chronic poverty or job shortages in your area. Remember Tenets 6 and 8, however: We must accept responsibility, and we can only grow when we are part of something greater. You cannot control national economic conditions, but maybe it lies within your power to do something that helps someone struggling with homelessness.

For example, if you are a business owner and need a job done, maybe you can give someone down on their luck a chance to turn things around for themselves. If you have the time, maybe you can crowdfund a project that might improve the situation. Even if you don't have much time or many resources, you can still buy someone a sandwich to prevent them from starving. As Seneca wrote (2017/c.65 A.D.): "We should give as we would receive, cheerfully, quickly, and without hesitation; for there is no grace in a benefit that sticks to the fingers."

Next, let's talk about protesting and participating in larger social movements. Again, you might think that Stoicism is incompatible with these wider movements, given the success or failure of such movements is often beyond one individual's control. However, Stoicism doesn't let you off the hook that easily. You may not be able to control whether or not a movement succeeds, but you *do* control whether or not you give your time and effort to the cause.

Rather than thinking about possible outcomes you cannot control, think about doing the next right thing. Think about your values and what your concept of justice demands of you. If there is a cause that tallies with your principles, and you believe it is right to voice your opinion in protest, then don't be put off by the idea that the movement might fail. For the modern Stoic man, that's not the point: The point is that you acted virtuously and with integrity.

Indeed, there is a Stoic tradition of civil disobedience. Cato the Younger, one of the most famous Roman Stoics, took up arms in active rebellion to oppose the dictatorship of Julius Caesar. Helvidius Priscus, another Stoic and Roman senator, refused to be silent on the floor of the senate when warned by his emperor that he would be executed if he continued in his duty.

The ancient Stoics weren't afraid to stand up for what they believed in, whether this meant protesting or simply refusing to participate in a practice they saw as unjust. You should follow their example. Whatever justice means to you, do not sacrifice your understanding of virtue for convenience or an easy life. Stand up for your beliefs, live with integrity, and flourish.

Discovering Purpose

In the final section of this chapter, let's think about purpose.

By living virtuously, you will find that living well is a purpose in itself. By remaining true to your principles and demonstrating wisdom, courage, temperance, and justice in all your dealings, you will live a purposeful life and experience the eudaemonia of living well. However, when motivating yourself to live in accordance with these virtues, it can also be helpful to reflect on those things that you care about in the world so that you can understand your values and what you take justice to be.

As a self-reflection exercise, consider the following questions. When answering, think about how they connect to Stoic teaching, in particular the tenets and the cardinal virtues. Explore your own beliefs and values and gain a deeper understanding of your own purpose and nature.

- What are you passionate about? What do you love doing? What would you do with your time if money wasn't a factor?

- Who do you care about? Who do you love?

- What are your core values? Which of the four cardinal virtues most resonates with you?

- What are you good at? What can you do better than most other people?

- What kind of world do you want to see in the future? What societal problem would you most like to see fixed? What can you do about that problem?

By understanding your values and purpose, you can act toward that purpose in a more deliberate and constructive manner and live more virtuously.

Conclusion

Stoicism, ultimately, is about personal responsibility. The modern Stoic is asked to determine what elements of life he can control and which elements he cannot, and then he is directed to take full responsibility for the former. By living according to our nature as rational human beings, we control how we react and process external events and have the choice to respond in a way that is wise, courageous, just, and temperate. By choosing to respond with virtue, we are able to flourish in even difficult circumstances and experience eudaemonia for ourselves.

The modern Stoic man must take these lessons to heart. He must take responsibility for his behavior and be a man of integrity, standing by his values and beliefs. However, this doesn't mean he should strive to become the stereotype of an unfeeling, excessively self-reliant man. The modern Stoic man is self-reliant but not to excess. He controls his emotions, but he processes them and understands them, and, if it is virtuous to do so, expresses them. Rather than repress his emotions, he confronts them directly through self-reflection and works through his problems rather than burying his head in the sand. Moreover, he recognizes that no man is an island and reaches out to his fellow human beings for co-operation and companionship.

This, then, is your task. By reading this book, you have begun your journey into a life of Stoic living. However, this is only the beginning. Stoicism is a life of constant self-improvement, self-reflection, and self-challenge. You will need to show grit and perseverance in the face of external challenges and temptations and prove your inner worth to yourself. You will need to remain disciplined and motivated and remember the values and virtues that give you purpose.

Even if you do all that, however, recognize that sometimes you will fall short. None of us are perfect. The ideal Stoic life is something to strive for, but the ideal is not a bludgeon to attack reality with. You'll lose your temper from time to time, avoid an issue you should be confronting, or simply feel too demotivated on a given day and blow off your commitments. That's okay. Reflect on what happened, use this setback as an opportunity for growth, and do the next right thing. You'll be in good company. Marcus Aurelius constantly berated himself for his failures—probably too much, from a Stoic perspective—and he is one of the most famous Stoics to ever live. Don't let perfection be the enemy of progress.

In addition, continue to explore the philosophy of Stoicism. After this conclusion is a chapter on further reading, which you can use to expand your knowledge and understanding of Stoicism. Moreover, experiment with what works for you. Stoicism is not a religion, and its teachings are not set in stone. Continue to reflect on your own understanding of the cardinal virtues. Think about other virtues and whether they should be included in your own personal version of Stoicism. Continue the tradition of ancient philosophy and think deeply about how life is best lived.

This is just the beginning, but life is not about the destination. The journey of self-improvement is fulfilling enough. Good luck on your path and remember: Every misfortune is virtue's opportunity.

Further Reading

You can further explore the philosophy of Stoicism, and how it can be applied to daily life, through the books below. This reading list is not meant as exhaustive, so follow your curiosity wherever it may lead you.

Primary Sources

- Marcus Aurelius: *Meditations*

- Lucius Seneca: *The Moral Epistles*

Secondary Sources

- Ryan Holiday: The Obstacle Is the Way

- Ryan Holiday and Steve Hanselman: The Daily Stoic

- William B. Irvine: A Guide to the Good Life

- Massimo Pigliucci: How to Be a Stoic

- Donald Robertson: Stoicism and the Art of Happiness

- John Sellars: Stoicism

Glossary

- **4-7-8 breathing technique:** A breathing technique in which you inhale for 4 seconds, hold your breath for 7 seconds, and exhale for 8 seconds.

- **Active listening:** To be contrasted with passive listening; the act of demonstrating engagement and interest when listening in a conversation.

- **Affirmation:** A positive phrase spoken aloud to help motivate the speaker.

- **Algorithm:** A set of automated rules that websites use to connect users with what they are likely to engage with online.

- **Apatheia:** An ancient Greek term referring to a state of mind where you are in control of your emotions.

- **Artificial intelligence (AI):** A computer program capable of tasks historically thought reserved for human intelligence.

- **Body language:** The nonverbal communication cues displayed by our bodies.

- **Body scan:** A mindfulness technique where you direct your attention to different parts of your body.

- **Cardiovascular disease:** A disease of the heart.

- **Clickbait:** An article with a misleading headline designed to get you to click upon it.

- **Cognitive behavioral therapy (CBT):** A psychiatric treatment for common mental disorders, focused on changing patterns of behavior and thought to improve your emotional state.

- **Cognitive cycle:** A fundamental principle of CBT, which holds that thoughts, behaviors, feelings, and physical sensations are causally interrelated.

- **Cosmopolitan:** An ancient Greek term, meaning "citizen of the world."

- **Emotional intelligence:** The ability to pick up on and respond appropriately to emotional cues.

- **Emotional resilience:** Your emotional well-being and health, including your ability to regulate your emotions in response to stress.

- **Eudaemonia:** An ancient Greek term, referring to a state of flourishing and fulfillment.

- **Euthymia:** An ancient Greek term, referring to a state of serenity and inner calm.

- **Eyebrow flash:** The act of briefly raising your eyebrows to show engagement and interest.

- **High-intensity interval training (HIIT):** A form of exercise that involves high-intensity bursts.

- **Hypertension:** High blood pressure.

- **Glucose:** A simple sugar that is a good source of energy for the body.

- **Glycemia:** The level of glucose in the blood.

- **Gut microbiome:** A collective term referring to the micro-organisms present in the gastrointestinal tract.

- **Immune activation:** The activation of the immune system in response to invading pathogens.

- **Insulin:** A hormone used by the body to convert sugar (primarily glucose) into energy.

- **Intermittent fasting:** The practice of intermittently reducing your calorie intake, associated with positive health benefits.

- *Kathékon:* An ancient Greek term, referring to an act that appropriately corresponds to your nature.

- **Listicle:** An online article presented in the form of a list.

- **Memento mori:** A Latin phrase, meaning "remember you must die."

- **Mindfulness:** A practice focusing on improving your control of attention and grounding you in the present.

- **Negative bias:** The evolved innate bias of humans to attend closer to negative stimuli than positive stimuli.

- **Negative visualization:** The practice of mentally rehearsing negative events to build your resilience to them.

- *Oikeiosis:* An ancient Greek term referring to the expanding of your circle of concern.

- **Paralanguage:** Verbal communication that does not involve words, such as grunts or uses of "hm."

- **Paraphrasing:** The act of summarizing what another person has said in your own words to demonstrate you have been listening and empathizing with them.

- **Philosophical charity:** The practice of interpreting someone else's views as charitably as possible when criticizing those views.

- **Physical resilience:** Your physical well-being and health, including your ability to resist physical illness in response to stress.

- **Recontextualization:** The practice of breaking down phenomena into their conceptual parts, often designed to remove feelings of temptation or allure from that phenomenon.

- **Sleep hygiene:** The patterns of behavior that influence the quality and quantity of your sleep.

- **Social resilience:** Your social well-being, including your social support network that you can rely on in times of hardship.

- **SMART goals:** An acronym used as a shorthand for the idea that a goal should be specific, measurable, achievable, relevant, and time-bound.

- **Spiritual resilience:** Your spiritual well-being, including your ability to rely on your sense of purpose in times of stress.

- *Stoa Poikilê:* A site in ancient Athens where early Stoics congregated; the source of the word "Stoicism."

- **The view from above:** A self-reflection designed to improve your sense of perspective.

- **Toxic masculinity:** A stereotypical expression of masculinity that is antisocial or psychologically unhealthy.

- **Voluntary hardship:** The practice of deliberately exposing yourself to minor hardship to build your inner resilience.

References

Atakan, M. M., Li, Y., Koşar, S. N., Turnagöl, H. H., & Yan, X. (2021). Evidence-based effects of high-intensity interval training on exercise capacity and health: A review with historical perspective. *International Journal of Environmental Research and Public Health 18*(13), 7201. DOI: 10.3390/ijerph18137201.

Aurelius, M. (2006). *Meditations* (M. Hammond, Trans.). [Originally written 161-180 A.D.]. Penguin Classics.

Camargo, C. Q. (2020, January 21). *YouTube's algorithms might radicalise people—but the real problem is we've no idea how they work.* The Conversation. https://theconversation.com/youtubes-algorithms-might-radicalise-people-but-the-real-problem-is-weve-no-idea-how-they-work-129955

Chatmon, B. N. (2020). Males and mental health stigma. *American Journal of Men's Health 14*(4). DOI: 10.1177/1557988320949322.

Cherry, K. (2023, May 2). *Emotional intelligence: How we perceive, evaluate, express, and control emotions.* VeryWell Mind. https://www.verywellmind.com/what-is-emotional-intelligence-2795423

Conlon, B. (2022, June 4). *Stoicism and love.* Medium. https://medium.com/stoicism-philosophy-as-a-way-of-life/stoicism-and-love-fda9416756b5

Dispatch Health Staff. (2019, April 29). *How depression affects your immune system.* https://www.dispatchhealth.com/blog/how-depression-affects-your-immune-system/

Epictetus. (2008). *Discourses and selected writings* (R. Dobbin, Trans.). [Originally written c.108 A.D.]. Penguin Classics.

Firth, J., Gangwisch, J. E., Borsini, A., Wootton, R. E., & Mayer, E. A. (2020). Food and mood: How do diet and nutrition affect mental wellbeing? *BMJ 369*. DOI: https://doi.org/10.1136/bmj.m2382

Gupta, S. (2023, June 9). *Why honesty is so important, according to a relationship expert.* VeryWell Mind. https://www.verywellmind.com/why-honesty-is-so-important-according-to-a-relationship-expert-7503996

Hall, J., Pennington, N. & Holmstrom, A. (2021). Connecting through technology during COVID-19. *Human Communication & Technology 2*(1). DOI: https://doi.org/10.17161/hct.v3i1.15026.

Hanselman, S. (n.d.). *The 9 core stoic beliefs.* Daily Stoic. https://dailystoic.com/9-core-stoic-beliefs/

Holiday, R. (n.d.). *10 insanely useful Stoic exercises.* Daily Stoic. https://dailystoic.com/10-insanely-useful-stoic-exercises/

Holiday, R. (2014). *The obstacle is the way.* Portfolio.

Holiday, R. & Hanselman, S. (2016). *The daily Stoic.* Profile Books.

Irvine, W. B. (2008) *A guide to the good life.* Oxford University Press.

Laertius, D. (2018). *Lives of the eminent philosophers* (J. Miller, Ed. & P. Mensch, Trans.). [Originally written in the 3rd century AD.]. OUP USA.

Llopis, G. (2012, July 17). *Great management boils down to one major thing.* Forbes. https://www.forbes.com/sites/glennllopis/2012/07/17/great-management-boils-down-to-one-major-thing/?sh=10507b9b2204

McRaven, W. H. (n.d.). *Make your bed* [Transcript]. JamesClear.com. Original speech given in 2014. https://jamesclear.com/great-speeches/make-your-bed-by-admiral-william-h-mcraven

Moore, A., Grime, J., Campbell, P., & Richardson, J. (2012). Troubling Stoicism: sociocultural influences and applications to health and illness behaviour. *Health* *17*(2). DOI: https://doi.org/10.1177/136345931245117.

Mosley, M. (2018). *The fast 800*. Short Books Ltd.

Namie, G. (2021). *2021 WBI U.S. workplace bullying survey*. Workplace Bullying Institute.

Neilson, S. (2019, July 25). *A warm bedtime bath can help you cool down and sleep better*. National Library of Medicine. https://www.ncbi.nlm.nih.gov/search/research-news/3495/

Nickerson, C. (2023, February 15). *The Yerkes-Dodson law of arousal and performance*. Simply Psychology. https://www.simplypsychology.org/what-is-the-yerkes-dodson-law.html

Nunez, K. (2019, August 19). *Is sleeping on the floor good or bad for your health?* Healthline. https://www.healthline.com/health/sleeping-on-the-floor

Ohrnberger, J., Fichera, E., & Sutton, M. (2017). The relationship between physical and mental health: A mediation analysis. *Social Science & Medicine* *195*, 42-49. DOI: https://doi.org/10.1016/j.socscimed.2017.11.008.

Pew Research Center. (2023, July 12). *Voter turnout, 2018–2022*. https://www.pewresearch.org/politics/2023/07/12/voter-turnout-2018-2022/

Pigliucci, M. (2017). *How to be a Stoic*. Rider.

Psychology Today Staff. (n.d.). *Resilience*. Psychology Today. https://www.psychologytoday.com/gb/basics/resilience

Rippe, J. M. & Angelopoulos, T. J. (2016). Relationship between added sugars consumption and chronic disease risk factors: Current understanding. *Nutrients 8*(11), 697. DOI: 10.3390/nu8110697.

Robertson, D. (2018). *Stoicism and the art of happiness.* Teach Yourself.

Robertson, C. E., Pröllochs, N., Schwarzenegger, K., Pärnamets, P., Van Bavel, J. J., & Feuerriegel, S. (2023). Negativity drives online news consumption. *Nature Human Behaviour 7*, 812–822. DOI: https://doi.org/10.1038/s41562-023-01538-4.

Rolls, B. J., Roe, L. S., Beach, A. M., & Kris-Etherton, P. M. (2012). Provision of foods differing in energy density affects long-term weight loss. *Obesity Research 13*(6), 1052-1060. DOI: https://doi.org/10.1038/oby.2005.123.

Scott, A. J., Webb, T. L., James, M. M., Rowse, G., & Weich, S. (2021). Improving sleep quality leads to better mental health: A meta-analysis of randomised controlled trials. *Sleep Medicine Reviews 60.* DOI: 10.1016/j.smrv.2021.101556.

Scott, E. O. (2016, October 29). *Stoics do care about social justice: A response to Irvine.* Modern Stoicism. https://modernstoicism.com/stoics-do-care-about-social-justice-a-response-to-irvine-by-eric-o-scott/

Sellars, J. (2006). *Stoicism.* Routledge.

Seneca, L. (2017). *The moral epistles* (R. M. Gummere, Trans.). [Originally written c.65 A.D.]. CreateSpace Independent Publishing Platform.

Shpancer, N. (2021, September 1). *Why you should talk to strangers.* Psychology Today. https://www.psychologytoday.com/gb/blog/insight-therapy/202109/why-you-should-talk-strangers

Slavich, G. M., & Irwin, M. R. (2014). From stress to inflammation and major depressive disorder: A social signal transduction theory of depression. *National Institutes of Health 140*. 774-815.

Spar, M. (n.d.). *What does it mean for a man to be stoic?* https://drspar.com/what-does-it-mean-for-a-man-to-be-stoic/

Stibich, M. (2020, December 15). *SMART goals for lifestyle change.* VeryWell Mind. https://www.verywellmind.com/smart-goals-for-lifestyle-change-2224097

The Associated Press. (2023, August 10). *Suicides in the U.S. reached all-time high in 2022, CDC data shows.* NBC News. https://www.nbcnews.com/health/mental-health/cdc-data-finds-suicides-reached-time-high-2022-rcna99327

Thomson, J. (2021, October 15). *The power to choose: How stoicism approaches toxic relationships.* Big Think. https://bigthink.com/thinking/stoicism-toxic-relationships/

Torrens, K. (2023, July 18). *Top 10 health benefits of fasting.* BBC Good Food. https://www.bbcgoodfood.com/howto/guide/health-benefits-fasting

Vaish, A., Grossman, T., & Woodward, A. (2008). Not all emotions are created equal: The negative bias in social-emotional development. *Psychological Bulletin 134*(3), 383–403. DOI: 10.1037/0033-2909.134.3.383.

Warburton, D. E. R., Nicol, C. W., & Bredin, S. S. D. (2006). Health benefits of physical activity: The evidence. *Canadian Medical Association Journal 174*(6), 801–809. DOI: 10.1503/cmaj.051351.

Watson, K. (2017, April 25). *Cold shower benefits for your health.* Healthline. https://www.healthline.com/health/cold-shower-benefits

Welton, S., Minty, R., O'Driscoll, T., Williams, H., Poirier, D., Madden, S., & Kelly, L. (2020) Intermittent fasting and weight loss. *Canadian Family Physician 66*(2), 117–125.

Wong, Y. J., Owen, J., Gabana, N. T., Brown, J. W., McInnis, S., Toth, P., & Gilman, L. (2016). Does gratitude writing improve the mental health of psychotherapy clients? Evidence from a randomized controlled trial. *Psychotherapy Research 28*(2), 192–202. DOI: 10.1080/10503307.2016.1169332.

Worley, S. L. (2018). The extraordinary importance of sleep. *Physical Therapy 43*(12), 758–763.

Image References

Dall-E. (2023, October 14). *The Stoic Man's Guide* [Images]. Dall-E. https://openai.com/dall-e-2

Made in the USA
Middletown, DE
30 January 2024